INSTRUCTIONAL MEDIA CENTER

Bold New Venture

INSTRUCTIONAL
MEDIA CENTER

Bold New Venture

EDITED BY

HAROLD S. DAVIS

INDIANA UNIVERSITY PRESS

BLOOMINGTON AND LONDON

Published in Canada by Fitzhenry & Whiteside Limited
Don Mills, Ontario

Library of Congress catalog card number: 73-143244
ISBN: 0-253-33010-6

Manufactured in the United States of America

THIS BOOK IS DEDICATED TO DAVID W. BEGGS, III to whom we owe so much. It was his dream that a series of books providing a symposium of contemporary, down-to-earth thinking be developed for each of the major areas of innovation. His brain child, "The Bold New Venture Series," was begun and is being continued by the Indiana University Press.

This book, the latest in that series, is also a tribute to his widow, JOAN BEGGS, who has helped to keep the idea alive. It was she who preserved Dr. Beggs' original notes and made the opening chapter possible.

Those who knew Dave Beggs realize that he was a rare combination of practitioner and theorist. His book *Decatur-Lakeview High School: A Practical Application of the Trump Plan* describes the school program that he developed and certainly establishes his place as one of the pioneers in the development of the modern IMC.

H.S.D.

Preface

Bold New Venture Series

AMERICAN EDUCATION is emerging as a new frontier. Staggering challenges brought about by the contemporary demand for quality education for a bulging and diverse student population must be met. Old solutions for new problems will not suffice.

Pioneer educators are testing promising new programs and practices to effect fundamental improvement in the schools. Healthy dissatisfactions have led to the belief that if the schools are to be significantly better, they will have to be substantially different. Both the substance and the form of instruction are undergoing searching reappraisal. Exciting innovations have been instituted in schools scattered throughout the country. The *Bold New Venture* series is designed to inform educators and the interested public about these new developments and to assist in their evaluation.

The books in this series differ from much of the professional literature in education. The contributors, for the most part, are practitioners. Admittedly they are partial to their topics. Nevertheless, pitfalls are exposed and candid treatment is given to the issues. Emphasis has been put on reporting *how* as well as *why* new practices and programs were inaugurated. The volumes in this series are intended to be a stimulus to the conversation which must take place if fresh methods of teaching are to find their way into the schools.

Topics included in the *Bold New Venture* series include team teaching, flexible scheduling, independent study, the nongraded school, instructional materials centers, data processing, small group instruction, and technological aids.

While journalists criticize, scholars theorize about, and philosophers analyze education, the teachers of America must act. Educators must leap from theory to practice in individualizing instruction. More responsibility must be given and accepted by youngsters for their own learning. Intellectual inquiry must become full-time, leisure-time, and life-time pursuits.

Progress in education does not always come by the process of addition with more teachers, more books, more courses, and more money. Real improvement can come from original uses of scarce human talent, precious time, and new methods.

Because it is intended primarily for teachers and administrators, the *Bold New Venture* series focuses on the practical problems of teaching. What has been operationally successful for some teachers may have application for other teachers. If new practices or programs result from these books, then the series will have fulfilled its aim, for the *Bold New Venture* books are calls and guides to action.

EDWARD G. BUFFIE

Bloomington, Indiana

Contents

PART IV
THE SUMMARY

Introduction

DYNAMIC NEW TRENDS can be identified readily in both elementary and secondary school education. Some changes are related to the curriculum and others to how instruction is given. Until recently, most of the focus has been on content; for example, modern mathematics and new science materials. But new materials require new methods, and, thus, the emphasis has begun to shift. Principals and teachers are asking searching questions: How can the schools give better instruction? How can the individual competencies of teachers be maximized? How can the school organization be improved? How can instruction be individualized? How can learning be improved?

In the attempt to leap from theory to practice, new ideas have been introduced. Nongraded programs, variable class sizes, independent study, flexible scheduling, and the growth of special remedial and developmental programs all are aimed at individualizing instruction. Each of these programs requires the student to use more instructional materials than have been used traditionally in schools. The establishment of a storehouse of information is no longer adequate. Today, a materials laboratory is required for every school. Such a laboratory contains both a wide range of information in diverse forms and the space and equipment for students to work individually and in small groups. Such a facility is an instructional media center.

Another contemporary educational trend places more emphasis on student involvement in learning. For example, youth are asked not only to learn about science, but to actually conduct scientific investigations. Working on experiments is no longer a once-a-week task. Instead, using the methods of independent scientific investigation is a continuing process. Foreign language provides a second example. The emphasis is placed on the student's own activity rather than on the memorization of vocabulary and structural forms. Students learn the language by associating objects they know with the words. They learn by listening to, and by speaking in, the new language. A third example is in the field of social studies. New methods at all age levels require the student to gather information, to make discriminating judgments concerning complex conceptual relationships, and to think through knotty global issues. Additional examples could be cited in reading instruction, English, mathematics, and the practical and fine arts, all of which put new emphasis on involving the learner.

Teaching and talking are no longer considered synonymous. The new methods of instruction clearly place added responsibility on the learner. As part of this responsibility, new techniques require the student to use varied approaches and to carry on diverse study activities. Sometimes he will need to read; sometimes question a teacher; and at other times listen to electronic tapes of explanations or to original recordings of events. Both varied materials and appropriate work spaces must be provided for such activities. Schools must be stocked with more materials for learning than previously thought necessary. Books with differing views, intellectual complexities, and reading levels are being provided for today's youth. Pamphlets, paperbacks, and magazines are necessities, not frills. Films, filmstrips, electronic tapes, records, language laboratories, photographic slides, mock-ups, transparencies, programed learning, and teaching machines are part and parcel of the learning process. The text is no longer "the Bible" for any course. Teachers use a variety of technological devices: overhead projectors, videotapes, television, and language labs. However, these aids to learning need to be organized in a systematic manner within a school if they are to be used productively and systematically. This cannot be done effectively unless we realize that the IMC is more than a repository for books and other media. It must be a place where *services* emanate and flow out into the classrooms, schools, and homes of the community. For this reason the IMC should be staffed by professionals capable of handling the complex problems of acquiring, organizing, and utilizing all types of instructional media.

Responsible educators will want to give serious consideration to the establishment of an instructional media center in every elementary and secondary school building.

The Concept Refined

The instructional media center or IMC is sometimes referred to as the instructional materials center, educational resources center, educational services center, library-AV center, or learning materials center. It is the place where ideas, in their multimedia and diverse forms, are housed, used, and distributed to classrooms and laboratories throughout the school. The IMC contains books, magazines, pamphlets, films, filmstrips, maps, pictures, electronic tapes, recordings, slides, transparencies, microforms, and learning programs. But to list the contents of the IMC is to give an incomplete description of this vital part of the school program. The most important aspect of an IMC is the use that both students and teachers make of it. The highest level of importance is related to what people do, not to the things at hand.

The IMC is more, much more, than a storehouse of information in various forms. It is a work center for both students and teachers, a place for activity, and a place for quiet study. It is a service bureau designed to enhance the teaching-learning process.

This Book

This book is divided into four sections. The first deals with the theoretical concept. The second section points up practical aspects of establishing and operating an IMC. The third gives descriptions of outstanding instructional media centers. The final section provides a synthesis and a bibliography.

This book will have served its purpose if it becomes a guide to discussion for directors of instructional media centers, teachers, and school administrators as they delve into the promise and problems of the instructional media center.

INSTRUCTIONAL MEDIA CENTER

Bold New Venture

PART I

THE CONCEPT DEFINED

CHAPTER 1

Storehouse and Laboratory

by

DAVID W. BEGGS, III

*David W. Beggs, III was the principal of Lakeview High
School, Decatur, Illinois, when the Decatur-Lakeview Plan,
a flexible-scheduling team-teaching program, was inaugurated. He was a curriculum consultant for 16 school districts,
conducted workshops and institutes for teachers, wrote articles on team teaching for professional journals, edited several books in the* Bold New Venture *series, and authored the
book* Decatur-Lakeview High School: A Practical Application of the Trump Plan.

*Dr. Beggs was working with the senior high school of In-
diana University's laboratory school at Bloomington, Indiana, when he met an untimely death in an automobile accident.*

EDUCATORS WHO ESTABLISH AND PROBABLY USE an instructional media
center are demonstrating that they are getting their *doing* up to date
with their *knowing*. The IMC is an operational manifestation that
students learn from various sources, not from the single text alone
even when supplemented with information provided by teachers. The
instructional media center, when properly organized, is the heart of
the school. Rather than being only a place where ideas and facts are
stored in printed, recorded, and illustrated forms, the IMC is a beehive of activity. Both students and teachers use the IMC—students
for learning and teachers for designing and developing learning experiences.

2

Students learn from various sources in the IMC.

The instructional media center is the place where the broadest possible range of information in multiple and diverse forms is stored and readily available for use by both partners in instruction, the student and the teacher. Students can go to the IMC to read, listen, write, view, and construct. The IMC houses a wide range of books in terms of subject and complexity, along with pamphlets, magazines, newspapers, and mimeographed materials. Records, electronic tapes, photographic slides, transparencies, maps, posters, charts, mock-ups, models, teaching machines, films, and filmstrips are included. Necessarily, the center has the appropriate equipment for using all types of materials. Book and non-book media, appropriate to the age and/or the reading level of every student in the school, are properly included. The IMC is a place where there is much for everyone.

Too often the establishment of a richly stocked instructional media center is promoted as a means of making teaching easier. In reality the converse is true. A well-stocked instructional media center places unyielding pressures on the textbook-bound classroom teacher as students ask questions triggered by ideas gathered in the IMC.

Teachers who work in schools with a good instructional media center will want to suggest various data sources appropriate to both the interests and abilities of individual students. The IMC gives the teacher a fund of resources from which to draw in prescribing personalized learning activities and citing appropriate references to individual interests. This rich resource cannot be used adequately in instruction unless the teacher is aware of its holdings and knowledgeable about what a particular student needs to know to develop sharper understandings and keener insights. Thus school administrators must provide time for the teacher to explore all of the school's equipment, references, and tools. Whatever their form, instructional materials owned by the school are common property. The provincial notion that a teacher or department has exclusive use of any material is antagonistic to the underlying philosophy of the instructional media center.

The IMC which is developed cooperatively by the faculty has far more chance of being used fully than one organized by a compact between the librarian and the principal. If the IMC concept is to be translated into reality in a school, the faculty must have a genuine and functional interest in its development. Asking teachers to suggest holdings is not enough. It is mandatory to involve teachers in developing the philosophy of the center as it is organized: the policies which dictate why it is to be established; how it is to be used; and when students and teachers may use it.

The Process of Education

In a real sense, the establishment of an instructional media center is an operational manifestation of the faculty's belief that people learn as a result of their own activities. The IMC has provision both for quiet learning activities—reading, writing, listening, and viewing—and for learning activities which generate noise—discussion and typing. At appropriate times both noise-generating and quiet activities will be required.

Those who believe that one can learn much by himself will view an IMC as an imperative for the school. Important as logical, dynamic, and explicit presentations by teachers may be, lectures cannot constitute the sum of an education. They need to be coupled with involvement by the student in using or reusing the concepts presented in a formal class. The IMC provides the data sources, the space, and, where appropriate, the technological materials to make real learning possible.

"To learn or not to learn" is a question that each student must answer for himself. His answer in part is dictated by the availability of resources, personal assistance, and time available for his own work. The IMC can provide the place for easy access to a wide range of resources and for personal assistance from a teacher, but the school schedule must devote some segment of the day for the student to work on his own.

If education's aim is to develop in the individual a desire to learn, then the experiences students can have in the IMC are in concert with that aim. On the other hand, if the substance of education is to be found in a fixed body of information, in a few highly developed skills, or in indoctrination to a single view, there is little need for an instructional media center.

What Is the IMC?

The main catalog and related cataloging services should provide clear and meaningful guides to all learning resources in the school. The catalog contains entries for the school's books, pamphlets, charts, programmed learning materials, maps, and all other printed materials; school-owned discs, tape recordings, films, pictures, and other audiovisual materials. Some of these tools for learning will be housed in the IMC; others will be listed in the catalog but located in the laboratories and resource centers throughout the school. Materials located outside the IMC can be used by all the educational partners if the catalog notes where they are housed.

Too often schools have a rich fund of materials stored in obscure places with unfortunate restrictions on their use. Students should be able to hear and see information as well as to read it. The full resources of the school should be available to every student wherever he needs them. It is better to have books and equipment wear out from use than from old age!

However, the instructional media center is more than a storehouse. The center is a place for students to work. Sometimes the work will involve reading and at other times it will involve listening, viewing, and discussing. The IMC should be arranged so that reading, listening, and viewing can be done with ease, and the student must be free to shift from one to the other. Unlike the monastic silence of the traditional library, the IMC is a place characterized by varied activity.

The instructional media center will have a variety of equipment—typewriters, tape recorders, projectors, art and project construction materials. The IMC will be a beehive of activity when it is opera-

Students listen to original recordings of significant speeches.

tional. To make possible silent reading and careful thought organization there will be a quiet zone. To accommodate other types of work there will be a noise zone.

Teachers desiring to make learning prescriptions for students will find the center's resources invaluable. For example, youngsters with reading disabilities may listen to electronic tapes or disc recordings that explain basic concepts. Still other youngsters will listen to original recordings of significant speeches. The meaning of Shakespeare's plays will be enhanced when students listen to the world's great actors present them. Students will read original newspaper descriptions and see documentary film footage of the bombing of Hiroshima rather than rely on textbook accounts only.

Learning Theory and the IMC

Establishing an IMC implies that a faculty believes that students learn from active participation. The center promotes this view by providing both materials and space for activity. Furthermore, the IMC concept implies that understanding is developed through appeal to the senses of seeing and hearing.

Much of the learning students do is an outgrowth of class activity. The stirring lecture or the stimulating discussion contributes to the desire for additional knowledge. The IMC is the place where students satisfy their need to know, where learners internalize their understandings. The IMC also recognizes that youngsters can and should learn at varying rates and on different levels. Thus, there is a range in the complexity of materials. A student's pace as he goes through his study of a topic is limited only by his ability, interest, and time.

Implications for Scheduling

The class schedule on which the school operates indicates how the faculty thinks boys and girls learn. For instance, those educators who structure a school day in which students are given generous amounts of time for independent study have a view of how learning takes place different from the view of those educators who keep students largely immobile in class groups all day.

The IMC is a requirement for schools operating a varying class size schedule. In such a schedule students spend a portion of their day in large-group instruction of up to 150 students, a portion in small-group discussions of 8 to 15 students, and a portion in independent study. During the independent study time the IMC should be available for students to use as they see fit.

Certainly, the archaic practice of keeping pupils fastened to seats in a classroom or study hall must give way to increased flexibility and freedom. The practice of requiring a permit to go to the IMC is counter to its purpose. Freedom to find, ease to use, and stimulation to seek are hallmarks of the IMC.

A New Arrangement of Space

The IMC should be located to give easy access to its many resources. Often it is in the center of the building, in the middle of the school's traffic. The recognition that diverse activities will go on in the functioning IMC means that adequate space must be provided and arranged in functional ways. Areas are needed where students can read without interruption, type, work on teaching machines, view filmstrips, or listen to recordings at any time. Careful planning of individual and group work spaces in quiet and noise zones will make this possible.

While it is difficult to generalize about space requirements, the IMC needs to be far bigger than a traditional school library. Certainly there is justification for an IMC that is larger than a gymnasium. Independent study ought to have a higher priority in space allocation than basketball. The center should be of sufficient size to accommodate the maximum number of pupils who will use it at any given time. For example, if a school of 1,000 students is to be organized so that students will spend 30 percent of their time in independent study, the center should be able to handle 300 students. Division of the space within the IMC will vary in schools according to the kinds of learning activities that are to be available.

Creative and thoughtful planning of facilities should precede any building remodeling or new construction. A few years ago special rooms were provided for students to listen to recordings. Today, however, many schools prefer built-in record players with attached headsets. This arrangement requires less space and expense than special acoustical rooms and, at the same time, makes it possible for several students to listen to a single recording at one time.

Instructional media centers use individual carrels more often than tables for four to eight. A table for four or more students is a built-in communications center; it belongs in seminar rooms. A student has a right to a place to study in the center without the distraction of someone at his elbow or across a table.

Placing the spirit duplicator and the mimeograph machines in the center will insure teacher traffic and stimulate the use of materials. There is good sense in locating teachers' offices and workrooms adjoining the IMC, thereby bringing teachers, students, and materials close together. There will be more teacher-student conferences if teachers make themselves accessible. Furthermore, teachers can give constructive supervision if they work in the area where students are studying. Teaching by example is more effective than teaching by direction.

Every Staff Member's Business

Orientation of teachers to the philosophy and operation of the IMC deserves priority. The center is more than a library; teachers need to understand this. It is hoped that the teachers and the center staff will jointly select course content and structure learning experiences. Then

Instructional media centers provide individual learning carrels.

A student can study without distraction at an individual carrel.

students will use the center in studying diverse routes to solve a problem.

Administrative edict and a rearrangement of facilities alone will not cause the center to fulfill its purpose. An intensive on-the-job education program is necessary. Staff meetings aimed at familiarizing teachers with the IMC will go a long way toward insuring its use and integration into the teaching-learning processes.

Bibliographies prepared by the IMC staff are helpful, but there is good reason to provide some special time, perhaps in the pre-school orientation week or during institute days, when teachers, too, can prepare bibliographies. After each teacher has been through the stacks, studied the community resource file, listened to tapes and records, and viewed films, the IMC staff can prepare course lists, secure in the knowledge that the teacher has a general knowledge of what is on hand and where it is located. Teachers should be encouraged to contribute suggestions for additions to the center's holdings. Each staff member should have a sense of ownership of the IMC.

The school administrator needs to exercise positive leadership in developing solid understandings of the importance of the center. The IMC shouldn't grow like Topsy. It needs frequent and sustained attention by the building principal, including evaluation of the operation, of personnel, of procedures, and of contents.

Individualized Instruction

The IMC is a manifestation of the belief that *individuals* are taught, not *subjects*. The center is the place where every student—each with different ability—can go to learn at his rate and on his level of understanding. He can select any one of several methods of learning. As the IMC comes into its place in the school, teachers will depart from the single text to allow the goal of individualized instruction to become a reality.

Students should be given freedom to pursue diverse learning activities. When students get satisfaction from their work, control problems are minimized. In their studying, readers should read; nonreaders should listen or look; notebook constructors should paste, cut, and arrange. The most appropriate style for each student to learn should be his path to understanding. In this case the means is not as critical as the end. Personal success, so necessary for fanning the flames of inter-

The student learns at his rate and on his level of understanding in the IMC.

est in learning, can be every youngster's experience as he works in the IMC.

A Bench Mark of Excellence

For generations we have taught as we were taught, largely by listening to the teacher. Yet we know this makes for less efficient learning than when students are highly involved and active in the learning process. New curricula, improved patterns of organization for instruction, and the IMC are signs of the time. Every school, regardless of its size, has the beginnings of an instructional media center. Leadership is needed to harness its resources, point out its advantages, and get it into operation. The demands of this age require better and more learning. The establishment of an instructional media center is a means to this end.

CHAPTER 2

The Emergence of the Concept

by

DOROTHY A. MCGINNISS

Experience in several areas of library work has given Dorothy A. McGinniss a wide acquaintance with instructional media at various levels. She is presently an associate professor, School of Library Science, Syracuse University. She has worked with children in the Newark Public Library; with teachers at Southern Illinois University; as supervisor of library services, Baltimore County Board of Education in Towson, Maryland; and as executive secretary of the American Association of School Librarians.

Miss McGinniss has an M.S. in library science from Columbia University. For several summers she taught courses in school library work at Trenton State Teachers College and at Rutgers University.

History of the Concept

A PUBLICATION OF THE MINISTRY OF EDUCATION in England, records a statement from Ashton's Ordinances at Shrewsbury in 1578 that buildings should include "a library and gallerie for the said schools furnished with all manner of books, maps, spheres, instruments of astronomye and all other things apperteyninge to learning which may be either given to the schools or procured with the schools money." [1] Thus, we have evidence that the concept of the instructional media center does not belong exclusively to the twentieth century.

The periodical indexes are usually sensitive to the currency of a term and can give a fairly good indication of its usage. The *Educa-*

tion Index began using the subject heading "Instructional Materials Centers" in 1947. *Reader's Guide to Periodical Literature* has been using the heading "Instructional Materials Center" since 1959. *Library Literature* started to use the heading "Materials Centers" in 1952, and in March 1964 the heading "Instructional Materials Centers" was introduced. The articles listed under these various headings have grown steadily in number through the years.

Many school systems began thinking about IMC's years ago. As early as 1937 the Board of Education of Newark, New Jersey, recommended that the library and visual education departments be merged. For years many librarians have included materials other than books in their collections. In 1954 a publication of the Department of Audiovisual Instruction of the NEA seemed to envision just such a center. In 1956 the American Association of School Librarians made an official statement on the subject: "The American Association of School Librarians believes that the school library, in addition to doing its vital work of individual reading guidance and development of the school curriculum, should serve the school as a center for instructional materials."[2] The publication *Standards for School Library Programs,* issued by the American Library Association in 1960, included the preceding statement and was built around the concept of the library as an instructional materials center. In 1965–66 plans were set in motion for the updating of these 1960 standards. The publication resulting from these plans, *Standards for School Media Programs,* was published jointly by the American Association of School Librarians and the NEA Department of Audiovisual Instruction in 1969.

Some states now specify in their certification requirements the need for instructional materials specialists and in their school accreditation requirements the need for media centers. In the 1960 edition of the *Evaluative Criteria,* put out by the National Study of Secondary School Evaluation in Washington, D.C., Form F, which previously had dealt with the library, was titled "Instructional materials services —Library and audio-visual." Form F, which is used to accredit many high schools throughout the country, defines the instructional media center as "the school library and audio-visual department." It allows for the fact that these may be separate but seems to indicate that there should be some kind of centralization in terms of the needs of the school. Many colleges have begun to train instructional materials specialists rather than just librarians. Several Library Science Departments have become Instructional Media Departments. In some cases this change of label may indicate only awareness of the current fashion, but for others it means an expansion of the idea of school librarian and a willingness to accept new responsibilities.

Reports Available from Conferences

The increasing interest in instructional media centers has encouraged conferences and intensive study of the subject. In May 1962, the U.S. Office of Education, in response to many requests, held a three-day conference for state school library supervisors and library educators on the subject of the training necessary for specialists to work in instructional media centers. The proceedings of the conference are titled *The School Library as a Materials Center: Educational Needs of Librarians and Teachers in its Administration and Use.* In November 1963 the University of Illinois Graduate School of Library Science called a conference of all people interested in learning more about instructional media centers. The proceedings of this well-attended meeting are titled *The School Library Materials Center: Its Resources and Their Utilization.* A series of conferences was sponsored in 1963 by Alameda County State College in California under a Title VII grant of The National Defense Education Act on the subject of the training necessary for educational media specialists or those who would administer instructional media centers. In addition, educational associations are devoting more and more time to discussing the subject at their national meetings. Magazines are requesting articles about the concept and suggestions for putting it into practice. In January 1964 *Educational Leadership,* the organ of the Association for Supervision and Curriculum Development, devoted almost its whole issue to "Centers for Learning," another term for instructional media centers. The January 1966 issue of the *Bulletin of the National Association of Secondary School Principals* was devoted to the topic, "Libraries in Secondary Schools, A New Look." The concept of the IMC was carefully examined.

In 1963 the report of the NEA Project on Instruction included among its 33 resolutions for those who would improve their instructional program Resolution 28: "In each school system there should be one or more well-planned instructional materials and resources centers, consisting of at least a library and an audio-visual center. In each school building, there should be an instructional resources facility. These centers should be staffed by persons who are adequately prepared in curriculum and instruction in library service, and in audio-visual education." [3]

The Concept Defined

A most important consideration is exactly what is meant by the term "instructional media center." In an article in the *ALA Bulletin* in June 1955, Louis Shores stated the case very well and simply: "The Materials Center is an agency in our American schools responsible for the acquisition, organization and dissemination of all instructional materials used in the learning process." [4] Further in the same article he states that it is "not a replacement but an augmentation of the mission of the library." [5] In Form F of the *Evaluative Criteria* the job of the center is defined thus:

> The major purpose of the instructional materials center is to serve the established aims of the total educational program by (1) providing a rich variety of materials, recordings, still and motion pictures, filmstrips, and other audio-visual materials and resources, for use by teachers and students as individuals and in groups; (2) offering leadership in developing techniques for the use of various materials by teachers and students; (3) making available facilities, services, and equipment necessary for the selection, organization, and use of instructional materials; and (4) furnishing facilities for an assistance in the production of instructional materials and displays. [6]

In the 1956 Statement giving the philosophy of the American Association of School Librarians on the subject is this brief statement: "The function of an instructional materials center is to locate, gather, provide and coordinate a school's materials for learning and the equipment required for use of these materials." [7]

The purpose of such a center is expressed in a timely way by Dr. Amo DeBernardis, formerly assistant superintendent of the Portland, Oregon, public schools: "Just as the modern shopping center has made it easier for the shopper to buy things he needs without any waste of time and energy, so should the school system make it easier for the teacher to get the needed teaching tools by bringing together the various material, services, resources, and equipment into one center." [8]

In a speech at the American Association of School Administrators' Convention in Atlantic City in February 1964, Margaret Nicholsen, then head librarian at the Evanston (Illinois) Township High School, said: "An instructional materials center might be defined as a collection of print and nonprint materials and equipment so selected, arranged, located and staffed as to serve the needs of teachers and students and to further the purposes of the school. What can be housed in an instructional materials center will depend upon the physical facilities of the school and the staffing of the center. If the IMC has the space and staff, there is no reason why it could not handle any type of material or even supplies which would help students and teachers, as well as administrators." She listed the requisites for every instructional media center: books, filmstrips, maps, motion pictures, pamphlets, periodicals, phonograph records, slides, tapes, and the equipment necessary to use them. She mentioned other items which might be available depending upon staff and facilities: transparencies, realia, book copiers, laminating machines, tachistoscopes, portable public address systems, cameras, radios, television sets, typewriters, duplicators, language laboratories, and adding machines.[9] A listing of human resources and agencies in the community which could enrich the curriculum might also be included.

For efficient operation, such an IMC should be staffed by professionals who know materials of all kinds and who understand educational objectives, the curriculum, and methods of teaching. They should be supported by technical assistants who understand the machines and equipment necessary for the use of nonprint materials, and by clerical help who can free the professional staff for work with students and teachers.

Physical Features Important

If a media center is to function efficiently, certain physical facilities must be available. Space and furniture must be appropriate for group and class use as well as for individual use of all kinds of material. Materials and equipment must be stored so that they are easily accessible. The center must be equipped to list all materials and to circulate them easily and adequately.

An instructional media center should render many important services to a school. Materials suited to the needs of the school educational program and the individual needs of students and teachers should be carefully selected and efficiently and economically ordered. These materials should be organized adequately for maximum use, and teachers should be assisted in every way to enrich their teaching. Students should be made aware of varieties of materials and instructed in their use.

In an *NEA Journal* article entitled "School Libraries as Centers for Learning Experiences," Frances Henne of Columbia University summed up the services of an instructional media center very well.

The library staff, working with individuals, groups, and classes, guides and helps students to:

become intelligent users of all communication media;

develop good study and work methods and abilities for self-directed learning;

acquire and strengthen an interest in and liking for reading so that it becomes a lifetime source of information and pleasure;

acquire listening and viewing skills and appreciation;

analyze, interpret, and evaluate the materials of communication, and develop capacities for critical thinking and contemplation;

find books and materials that meet individual needs, interests, and abilities for class work and nonacademic purposes, and discover and explore new interests, ideas, and aspects of knowledge;

make wide use of the library's reference and guidance services;

understand and maintain desirable social behavior and attitudes.

The library staff assists teachers in these ways:

acquainting them with sources of materials and keeping them informed about materials appropriate to their teaching purposes;

providing professional materials covering developments in their special teaching fields as well as in the general area of education;

cooperating actively in the communication-arts program in such fields as reading readiness, individualized reading, developmental and remedial reading, and viewing and listening skills and appreciation;

working with them to implement a planned, sequential program of instruction on the use of library resources, integrated with classroom teaching;

serving as materials and resources specialists in curriculum planning and team teaching and continuously consulting with individual teachers about materials, special needs of students, and class group projects;

encouraging wide use of the library's reference and bibliographic services.[10]

Some educators and librarians apply the term instructional media center only to a system center; others use it to refer to either a system center or to a center in an individual school. Because the system center would be much more elaborate, some prefer to call it a learning resources center, a more inclusive term. Others would expand the more familiar term, library, to include the concept of the instructional media center. In this volume, the widely accepted term instructional media center is used. Regardless of semantics, the important consideration is that all types of materials be centralized for easy usage and that all the services mentioned here be easily available to students and teachers in every school.

Reasons for Instructional Media Centers

New developments have made instructional media centers essential to quality education. The explosion of knowledge has made it impossible to teach a subject thoroughly with the help of only one textbook. A teacher can touch on most important points, but then must encourage students to delve more deeply into the subject on their own. Students who are learning to be self sufficient must be taught how to find and use materials and must have plenty of opportunity to practice such activity in school situations under expert guidance.

An increasing emphasis on courses for the gifted requires materials and services that only a well-stocked and well-staffed instructional media center can supply. If the modern job of education is to teach students how to think and how to cope with conditions 20 years hence, they must learn about materials, how to find them, how to use them, and how to evaluate them. Teachers must teach for flexibility; students must learn how to learn. For this goal, good instructional media centers in suitable quarters with adequately trained staff are indispensable.

The NEA Project on Instruction emphasized two essentials for quality education: (1) the use of varied materials, (2) more individualized instruction for each child. One of the strong recommendations emanating from the project is that each school system should have a well-planned and adequately staffed instructional resources facility at the system center and in each school building. The report stated: "Students cannot learn on their own, either in school or later on, without instructional resources or knowledge of how to find and use them. Teachers need source material in order to plan creatively." [11] In another volume resulting from the project, *Planning and Organizing for Teaching*, the need for instructional media centers is stressed: "The resources offered will include not only books in abundance but also microfilms, charts, recordings, filmstrips, videotapes and other materials to whet the appetite for learning and to feed the hunger for understanding. In this sense the school library becomes the heart of a school's instructional services, pumping life-giving blood to the entire educational organism." [12] Here the word library is clearly synonymous with the term instructional media center as we have been employing it.

Making the IMC Function

Most educators recognize that the single textbook approach to learning is completely out of date and that the self-contained classroom cannot possibly furnish all the materials necessary for a good learning situation. In order to meet the needs of all children it is necessary to bring them in contact with the printed word in many forms at many levels of difficulty, to present ideas in pictures with and without sound, to use the oral approach through records and tapes, to utilize all kinds of educational media in the hope that at least one of the approaches will make an impression. To make these materials available for easy use is the objective of a good instructional media center.

It is necessary then to have this wealth of materials easily accessible to all teachers and students at the time when they can be most useful. The person in charge of the instructional media center must have the training in selection and in organization to function as coordinator and to see that the mechanics of organization are adequate. Each teacher, as a specialist in a particular field, can and should play an important role in the selection of materials, but often in the press of meeting large classes daily and preparing and correcting assignments, teachers cannot keep up with new publications. The educational media specialist, who has access to and knowledge of selection tools of all types, is therefore in a position to keep teachers informed of new materials. The mechanics of efficient, economical, and coordinated ordering can best be worked out by the specialist because he has been trained for this job and because he has contact with all the departments in the school. He can easily avoid unnecessary duplication of materials and relieve the teacher of the mechanics connected with ordering. The teacher can then devote more time to what he is best equipped to do.

Economy, Efficiency, Excellence, and Enrichment

Economy comes from centralized and careful buying under the supervision of a person skilled in the necessary methods and familiar with the entire school curriculum. There is also an economy of effort because teachers have one place where all their needs for materials can be met, and they can use the energy they save to do a better job of teaching. Efficiency results from organization and operation in well-planned facilities. In the right environment, students can accomplish their work much more satisfactorily, in a shorter time, and without frustration. Excellence refers to the service that can be given to teachers and students in an instructional media center. Enrichment is reflected in the whole educational program because teachers are helped to give their best efforts to the students, and the students become acquainted with all types of communication media and learn new techniques for acquiring knowledge.

CHAPTER 3

Instructional Media Programs and School Objectives

by

KENNETH I. TAYLOR

Kenneth I. Taylor is the assistant curriculum director for instructional materials for the Madison Public Schools, Madison, Wisconsin. He has worked with students at every grade level from kindergarten through graduate school, and he has taught at Florida State, Eastern Illinois State, and De-Paul universities.

Dr. Taylor is a workshop consultant for the U.S. Office of Education and has assisted in IMC design for many private and public schools around the nation. Among them was the West Leyden High School IMC, North Lake, Illinois, which gained national attention after opening in 1958.

THE PHENOMENAL PRODUCTION OF INSTRUCTIONAL MEDIA in recent years has caused a re-evaluation of the aims of education and the role of the teacher. Printed, pictorial, and audio symbols bring students more adequate understandings of domestic and international affairs than ever before possible. Children participate in dramatic events as they occur and later relive the events by means of recorded forms. New media have made it possible for a teacher to draw upon the talents of experts in every field. By skillfully introducing new resources into learning activities, the teacher can accomplish more with outside assistance than he could ever accomplish alone.

21

What We Have to Build On

In the past, the literature of visionaries bordered on science fiction, and the most sophisticated readers had difficulty determining whether what they were reading was still to come or was already an established fact. With the passage of only a few years, teachers see that they must continue to wait for the more fantastic predictions. Educators do not yet have the equivalent of the Library of Congress in every school. Students do not study entirely at home, nor do they attend teacherless schools. Neither do they identify themselves to teaching machines by their thumbprints.

Many new materials were marketed before their value had been determined, and the learning theories upon which they were based were often over-simplified or outmoded. Nevertheless, some instructional materials of great promise have been developed. The best of these new materials and equipment have fostered changes in teacher utilization, pupil activities, and building design. But the importance of the teacher has not diminished. The size of a class is still less significant than the careful definition of a teacher's instructional aims. The use of a motion picture instead of a television set is less important than an attitude the teacher encourages his pupils to develop. Decisions about the length of a class period pale against the evaluation of a student's behavior after he has studied, observed, and discussed the role of the citizen in community affairs.

The past decade has shown that instructional materials, from the day of Comenius' ingenious pictured text to the latest artfully programmed book, are most effective when used under the teacher's close direction. Instructional media are still a means to an end, not an end in themselves.

Renewed Emphasis on Use

The last decade has been significant for the teacher concerned with instructional materials because:

1. The variety and quality of materials available for his selection became greater than at any previous time.

2. Schools learned how to organize central media collections and services.

3. Educators began to concentrate not on administration but on instruction, not on media but on content, not on quantity but on quality, not on a singular but on multiple use, and not on teacher accessibility alone but also on student accessibility.

This renewed emphasis on use draws attention to the quality of instruction in every classroom, for the power of materials depends upon the precise definition of a teacher's major goals. When these goals are understood and when a student's growth is evaluated against them, instructional materials may be used most effectively.

Basic Objectives Are Timeless

Each generation has an idea of what it means to be an educated man. Educational programs are re-defined according to a generation's aspirations, its view of the nature of knowledge, its understanding of what young people need to know, and its theories of how pupils learn. Gardner writes that the American ideal of individual fulfillment is found in this nation's conviction concerning the importance of equality, the worth of every man, and his right to achieve the best that is in him.[1] To achieve this fulfillment, mid-twentieth-century children need individualized educational programs. The suggestion that science will provide mass systems, undifferentiated to meet the problems of the local community, becomes distateful; and educators search for methods by which technology, substantiated by conceptual research, more effectively individualizes each child's instruction.

Educators still view the ancient Socratic approach toward education, which encouraged the pupil's examination of his inner orientation toward life, as an ideal. They also see merit in the approaches of later teachers, such as Richard Mulcaster of the Merchant Taylor's school in London. Several of Mulcaster's principles, about which he wrote in 1581, seem strikingly modern:

1. The end and aim of education is to develop the body and the mind.

2. All teaching processes should be adapted to the pupil being taught.

3. The first stage in learning is of large importance and requires high skill on the part of the teacher.

4. The thing to be learned is of less importance than the pupil learning.[2]

Although American education has remained fairly constant in its basic objectives from colonial times to the present, methods have varied. A review of several early programs illustrates some of the contrasting methods that have been used by educators.

Survey of Past Methods

The American school in Colonial times began with highly individualized tutorial instruction. Students of different ages learned in the same room during the hours that could be spared from work at home. The few hornbooks and other religious and didactic materials were treasured and shared by many children.

In these early parish and dame schools, reading instruction was given priority over other studies, because it was assumed that every man should be able to read the Holy Scripture for his fullest development as a religious individual. Citizens believed in this goal and supported their schools through taxation. After the average student could read and master elementary ciphering skills, his education was considered to be reasonably complete.

The Lancaster-Bell plan of monitorial instruction, used more than 150 years ago, emphasized administration and organization and offered a means of educating the multitudes. First, a master teacher taught a small amount of information or a simple step in a computational skill to 10 students, whom he called his monitors. These students each taught ten others, each of whom in turn taught 10 more. Under this system, knowledge and skills were transmitted from a single teacher to as many as a thousand pupils, using monitors as communications media. Direct contact between teacher and pupil was abandoned in favor of mass education. In this early example of programmed instruction, the teacher structured a subject carefully and divided it so that it could be transmitted by his monitors. Each step was so minute that error by any student during its transmission was virtually eliminated. The same theory underlies today's programmed instruction. Modern adaptations present the steps in printed form so that not one thousand but hundreds of thousands of students are exposed to preplanned content. The printed medium allows each child to progress at his own rate, although what is studied is the same for all.

The revolutionary Quincy Grammar School of 1847 created smaller classes for greater contact between teacher and pupil. This classic building had classrooms of uniform size, one teacher per room, and pupils assigned to each room by age. Academic progress was patterned into grade standards, and each child either met them or failed to advance to another room. With the teacher's help, the pupil mastered materials and skills.

Although the small classes offered opportunities for individualized instruction, teachers could not ignore established standards and examinations. Therefore repetitive drill became the predominant method of instruction. Eventually, in its examination of 1873, the Quincy school committee discovered that its students were unable to read new selections at sight or to solve problems they had not previously studied. A re-evaluation of the entire school program was considered mandatory.

A slow reversal of the emphasis on uniform grade standards and rigid methods has preoccupied educators since that time. The best ideas of European teachers like Rousseau, Pestalozzi, and Froebel,[3] which focused on the individual development of children, were adopted. In addition to print, their schools had used field trips, drawings, toys, and three-dimensional models for visual and kinesthetic experiences. Naturally, American programs which incorporated such ideas were modified by the availability of materials.

Teaching Methods Affect Use of Materials

Methods used in these three early schools agreed with the contemporary ideas about knowledge and learning. Teachers in these schools were convinced that their methods gave individualized attention to each child. In the Colonial school, the adequacy of the tutorial approach in this respect is unquestioned. In the monitorial school, the master would have argued that each child received individual attention because he was taught alone by one of his classmates. In the Quincy school, each child was instructed until he met the standards for his grade, even if he took an extra year.

During the nineteenth century, knowledge was viewed as a stable resource, from which the educators selected the best of the past, occasionally adding new discoveries. The child's mind was regarded as an empty receptacle, and the teacher's job was to fill it as best he could. When the teaching method was intensive drill, the only materials necessary were the formulations of knowledge contained in the textbooks. Standard texts and workbooks, even if prepared by the teacher, were considered adequate for the average pupil. Additional materials were considered supplementary, intended for leisure or study beyond minimum requirements. However, supplementary collections were available in the earliest schools. Even for the mammoth monitorial school, the master teacher's manual recommended: "The school should have a collection of amusing and instructive books, to be chosen by the committee, which may be lent to the best pupils in the school as a reward for their good conduct. The library is placed upon a platform either at the side of or behind the master's desk." [4]

Children Learn in Different Ways

A review of early American schools reminds the contemporary teacher that some schools still reflect administrative practices and teaching methods that were popular a century ago. Some still operate as if knowledge and skills were transmitted exclusively by the teacher or the text. Outmoded administrative practices require elementary teachers to teach such varied subject matter that many experts would be needed to do the job well. Secondary teachers spend a full year on material that students could cover in less than half the time if the text were well written and supplemented with additional media. Children in such schools are being trained to follow directions from the teacher, text, or laboratory manual, and are required to study in exactly the same manner as their peers. Undoubtedly no school functions in this manner all the time in each classroom and at every grade level; but many give a disproportionate amount of this kind of nineteenth century instruction and do a serious injustice to a child's need for development.

Twentieth-century research indicates that differences among children of the same age are greater than educators had previously imagined. It has been shown that children learn in many different ways. Their perception of what is being taught is highly individualistic and is influenced by previous experiences inside and outside school. Some children learn primarily through role playing, demonstration, committee activity, and manipulation of three-dimensional models. Others, because of previous experiences and personal orientation, learn primarily through reading.

No single approach works for all. Teachers who accept this axiom must continue to create new learning activities for individualized instruction. It is clear by now that standard teaching has been effective only for those fortunate children who learn in spite of the method. Thousands of others who could learn equally well through visual and kinesthetic activities have failed to find valuable learning experiences in the schools.

Adapting instruction to each child is as difficult now as it was for previous generations. Teachers find the educative task becomes even more complex as children progress. The more effective the school program, the greater pupil differences become; and as differences increase, students need a greater variety of resources to use in pursuing their individual learning.

Instructional Objectives and Learning Activities

Classroom objectives should be specific enough to evaluate student growth. Tyler writes that they are most useful when they identify the behavior to be developed in the student and the content or area of life in which the behavior operates.[5]

The teacher creates learning activities which promise to lead the student to grow toward his objectives. Because he frequently has a choice of activities, he may select them in cooperation with his pupils. Within these activities or learning experiences, instructional materials are used. If materials are used in lieu of the activities themselves, inefficiency results.

Learning activities are simplified for initial student understanding of new ideas and concepts. For example, teachers can simplify the study of community problems by carefully organizing discussion of social issues to develop in each student a maximum degree of comprehension without creating the confusion of voices they will encounter as adults.

However, in this process of simplification, the teacher must not reduce the number of voices so greatly that students are dependent solely on the teacher's point of view or that of a single textbook

writer. To do so perpetuates student reliance on others and may reduce opportunities for developing critical thinking.

By encountering conflicting opinions through varied media, students develop wholesome skepticism to new ideas. This skepticism involves objectivity and willing suspension of one's commitment to an
idea or proposal until he has examined the backgrounds, motivations,
and perceptions of writers and speakers. It is an important step toward the maturity and self-assurance which are needed for personal
inquiry.

Media and Classroom Environments

It is the task of teachers to design controlled, contrived environments
so effective that students can learn at various levels of maturity.
Media centers, current collections, and professional services are
means by which classroom environments support a variety of learning
activities. Imagine, for example, a randomly selected sixth grade
room. By observing its books, charts, bulletin boards, globes, maps,
filmstrips, and picture files, a visitor can estimate to what extent the
classroom brings its students into contact with the outside world.

Ralph Ellsworth has described instructional materials as "carriers
of knowledge," [6] an appropriate term for self-contained media with
cognitive content. For active sources of live information such as radio
and television, the term "communication lines" suggests the direct
participation that students experience. Both static and active symbols
contribute to environments that are rich, effectively organized, and
well-suited for students.

Consider, for example, the striking difference between a home that
subscribes to no newspaper and one that receives several, or a home
that has no telephone and one that does. The illustration is analagous
to schools and classrooms. The variety and the quality of incoming
carriers of knowledge and communication lines provide an index to
the potential strength of a curriculum.

Reading Instruction and Multi-Media

For many years, libraries have made their greatest contributions
through the support of reading objectives and have become closely
identified with this aspect of instruction. Because research indicates

that audiovisual materials are necessary for well articulated, school-wide reading programs, it is logical to assume that the media center will most effectively support the school's total program if it retains the library's identity with reading as a basis for continued development and maturity.

Good reading programs are strengthened by central services and collections. In turn, reading programs will foster effective media centers if they have certain characteristics:

1. Reading programs extend from grades K through 12.

2. Reading is directly or indirectly taught at every grade level in every subject.

3. Reading instruction consists of planned experiences which combine viewing, listening, speaking, and writing.

4. Reading programs include personal and social activities, which require the facilities of the media center for individual and group study.

Research studies contain implications for audiovisual materials in reading instruction. At the first stages of reading, children are taught to read pictures to develop visual perception for distinguishing subtle differences among printed symbols. Gradually they move from the familiar to the unfamiliar in what they see. Models, still pictures, filmstrips, and motion pictures ease the transition from reality to the printed page by identifying the object with the symbol. Tape recorders develop auditory perception by relating sounds to letters and to combinations of letters in phonics, and they allow children to hear themselves as they pronounce words and read aloud. Tapes or records relate the spoken words to the printed text of a favorite story.

As children progress beyond basic words symbolizing concrete objects, they learn words of greater abstraction from varied media. Concepts are developed by seeing one topic through different media. Group discussion of these concepts reinforces the teacher's purpose and prevents the misunderstandings that are apt to result among children of contrasting backgrounds. Favorite children's stories on filmstrips and records introduce or review reading materials. Reading becomes a social as well as a personal experience.

Use of the media centers enables students to select their reading from a larger collection than the teacher can develop alone. Children select works of interest and then proceed at their own rates. This free study encourages exploration and discovery, a preliminary step to inquiry.

A fully developed reading program uses curricular principles found in other programs, such as sequential development, cyclical repetition of instruction, and opportunities for application of skills and understandings. As teachers relate instructional materials to reading programs, they should see similar relationships in other subjects. These relationships imply that the successful materials center will be less dependent on physical quarters and quantitative standards than on the program it supports.

Materials and Vicarious Experiences

To build common experiences among children, the elementary teacher may take a class behind the scenes of the post office. The high school teacher may take students to an industrial plant to explain labor-management problems. But, unless visits are carefully planned, pupils may develop inaccurate concepts. For example, a visit to the United Nations Building would not explain the kinds of human relationships involved in processes of international negotiation, nor the multitude of activities extending to every area of the globe. These things can be experienced better by a combination of sounds and visual images via television or motion pictures.

Then, too, a teacher cannot be expected to take students on visits to see everything they study or discuss. Yet, experiences must be provided by every classroom teacher. More than 20 years of studies involving students of various socioeconomic backgrounds indicate that youngsters who come from privileged environments are likely to be better readers and learners than those from poorer areas.[7] They have traveled greater distances, seen such things as newspaper plants, and met professional associates of their parents. They know more about vocations available to them in the future and the implications of world events. Audiovisual materials make it possible to provide vicarious experience for all in lieu of real experience for a few.

Faculty Development of School-Wide Media Programs

A media center implies a school-wide media program. It requires financial support and the professional and organizational ability of qualified consultants, faculty involvement, administrative leadership, and evaluation of almost all aspects of the curriculum.

A school can best begin its media program by relating its collections and services to one major area of instruction. Any subject of high priority may be selected, although it is wise to begin where a degree of early success can be assured. For this reason, schools might begin by relating the media center to the reading program. A number of factors make this a feasible area for initial study:

1. The reading program is well established in many classrooms.
2. Its value is apparent to most teachers.
3. A supply of reading materials is present.
4. Many opportunities for introducing audiovisual media are possible.
5. Background material for teachers has been published by many subject-area organizations, for example, the National Council for the Social Studies.
6. Tests for the evaluation of literary appreciation, general reading skills, critical reading and thinking, and knowledge of sources of information are readily available.
7. Basic instructional relationships among broad areas, such as English, social science, and science, are found through reading instruction.
8. Development of reading skills is indispensable to independent study.

As far as possible, instructional objectives in any subject should be defined in terms of student behavior. Skills in understanding, application, and evaluation are found in guides such as the *Taxonomy of Educational Objectives;* [8,9] The National Society for the Study of Education yearbook, *Measurement of Understanding;* [10] and the National Council for the Social Studies yearbook, *Skill Development in Social Studies.*[11]

The identification of objectives, understandings, and skills for a total school program gives teachers freedom to experiment with learning activities as well as the security of operating within a well-structured context. Within this context teachers cease to spend most of their time imparting information and begin to assist students in learning for themselves.

From Traditional Teaching to Creative Inquiry

Creative inquiry as an objective for every student has implications for media centers, teaching procedures, learning activities, and school design. It requires:

1. a student background of general and special knowledge;
2. easy access to additional sources of information;
3. a command of fundamental general and special skills for using knowledge;
4. an understanding of the more simple procedures of traditional inquiry;
5. opportunity to consult with others;
6. encouragement to include personal experience and novel ideas.

General and special knowledge commonly offered through the multi-copy laboratory manual, the programmed book, and the text, while fundamental, is insufficient. A variety of instructional media is required to solve individual problems at any moment. Consequently, schools must see that media centers are well stocked and accessible to all students. Opportunities to study alone and to consult with others must be provided during the school day. Creative inquiry, although solitary, often requires discussion and collaboration. Facilities and routines should accommodate small-group discussions, private conferences, and independent study.

Like their teachers, students should understand that what their school provides is elementary, subject to change and re-order, and preliminary to personal discovery. They should see that education begins by learning about how man has learned in the past, what he has found, and how he has organized what he has learned for the greatest utility and for transfer to others. Only a very limited sample of these past learnings can be given during the short time spent in school. To this sample must be added an acquaintance with reference sources to enable students to obtain additional knowledge.

The educator should see that a learner's active quest for information and the production of new ideas arise out of his immediate experiences.[12] Thus, the school should help students progress beyond the understanding, appreciation, and repetition of previous modes of discovery to active involvement in matters of personal interest and need. This process relates what the student has learned from core activities and from life. Conclusions of his efforts are personal and, at least to him, new.

The IMC will reach maturity only when its materials, services, and facilities support a school-wide program of creative inquiry. An intelligent combination of collective and individual learning activities guarantees that each student will receive a core of understandings and skills which he can adapt to his personal pattern of discovery.

Major educational goals remain basically the same, but methods of achieving objectives are changing rapidly. An accelerating accumulation of knowledge makes it difficult to select what is best for today's pupils. Modern discoveries frequently restructure subject fields and illuminate relationships that formerly were unseen. In a social order that undergoes radical changes within a decade, students and teachers must be prepared to unlearn and relearn without apprehension, to view education as a lifelong process, to accommodate social change, and to seek solutions to problems they have not yet encountered.

PART II

ORGANIZATION AND IMPLEMENTATION

CHAPTER **4**

The School Library in Transition

by

ALICE LOHRER

Alice Lohrer, who holds a doctor's degree from the University of Chicago, is a professor in the Graduate School of Library Science, University of Illinois. A former president of the Illinois Association of High School Librarians, she serves as a consultant for school libraries in Illinois and Missouri and directs library institutes and workshops in several states.

As the recipient of Fulbright and Rockefeller grants, Dr. Lohrer has lectured at universities in Bangkok, Thailand; Tokyo, Japan; and Teheran, Iran. She has published professional articles, co-authored books, and reviewed children's literature.

IN ANY ADMINISTRATIVE HIERARCHY the units within a system reflect the philosophy, the objectives, and the organization of the parent in stitution. This is as true of a media center as of a school library. The administrative patterns of school systems and of independent public and private schools in the United States directly affect the organization, the program of services, the staffing, and the type of resources considered the responsibility of the library in each school. Since the school library, unlike the public library, is not an entity in itself but an integral part of a school or a school system, prevailing organizational differences will be considered briefly as background for a more detailed look at instructional media centers themselves.

Patterns of School Organization

Unlike the centrally administered state educational programs in other countries, many organizational patterns of school systems and of independent schools are found in the United States. They are significantly different from each other. This is true at each level of the educational ladder and in each state, regardless of whether schools have grade level patterns on an 8-4, 6-3-3, or K-12 plan. This is because our federal constitution delegates responsibility for education to the states, and they, in turn, have delegated the responsibility to local communities.

At least one of our states, however, has a unified program of school organization. In Hawaii, the school system is administered as a unit. The director of school library and instructional services holds office at the state level and also works at the local school building level in a coordinating, supervisory, and advisory capacity for all public school libraries in Hawaii. The director's title is Program Specialist for School Library Services. This type of centralization of school library supervision has led to a more adequate program of library service in the schools and is bringing about greater equalization of facilities and materials among all schools. By working directly with the local schools and with program specialists in many subject areas, the school library director can play a dual role of leadership at both state and local levels.

A second pattern is found in some southern states where school administration is centralized at a county level. In Florida, Louisiana, North Carolina, and Tennessee, for example, the political unit known as the county or the parish is also the educational unit of the state. This results in centralization of administration in each unit of government, including the school. Excluding a few large metropolitan areas, a school superintendent is the administrative officer at the head of all public schools in that county. The supervisor, director, or coordinator of library services or of instructional media, whatever the title may be, is likewise responsible for all school libraries in the county or parish. Not all counties have a school library supervisory staff, but other supervisors can lead in planning and strengthening the programs of library service in each school.

Many states have been working for school consolidation, but the patterns of school administration and organization within each state vary greatly. In the majority of states, individual communities have been delegated the responsibility for educating their youth as they see fit. Most school systems in towns and cities have jurisdiction over both public elementary and secondary schools. In at least three states, however, there are separate township and district four-year high schools that are not part of the centralized elementary school systems that feed into them. In the states of Illinois, Arizona, and California, a town may have a school board for the elementary school system and a separate school board for the township high school. A school library consultant for the elementary schools may have no responsibility for the library service in the high school. In such cases cooperative projects could be undertaken, but they would be voluntary.

Some consolidated districts include urban and rural schools of all grade levels as part of a central school system. Ideally, there is a school library supervisor to develop a program of library service for the entire system. However, in some districts it is the high school librarian who assumes the responsibility of expanding the limited resources and services to include some services for the elementary schools. In still other areas no library service to elementary schools is provided by the school board. Federal aid to education is helping to improve this situation.

In some rural areas or sparsely settled areas in the mountain and plains states, schools are under the jurisdiction of a county school superintendent. The enrollment of these schools is usually small, and the library may be only a collection of books in a study hall or classroom.

School consolidation eliminating the inefficient one- and two-room schools and efforts to set a desirable minimum enrollment for high schools have brought about a series of interrelated changes, including an increase in library services and resources. With the elimination of small school units and the expansion of integration efforts, an increasing proportion of students are now transported to schools by bus. Often the bus schedules have an impact on school library services. Library schedules and services before and after school may be determined by the bus schedule rather than by the instructional needs of the students. Cognizant of this fact, some school systems plan the bus schedule to accommodate students who remain in school to use library facilities after school hours or who wish to return to the library in the evening or on Saturday. Also, increased attention is being given to the problem of extended hours of school library service. Without exception, school consolidation has led to the improvement of library services and resources where arrangements have been made for effective access to resources.

At the other end of the spectrum, recommendations for maximum enrollments for elementary, junior, and senior high schools have resulted in the construction of new school plants rather than additions to existing school buildings. The new school plants may be located in separate parts of a school district or on one campus. New campus schools usually have separate buildings for specialized programs of instruction planned for the shared use of all students, for example, the gymnasium, the auditorium, the cafeteria, and the instructional media center.

In a cross section of school systems the library quarters and programs would be as different as the academic and administrative patterns they reflect. The library may serve as the total instructional media center for a school, or the library and audiovisual programs may be separate though housed in the same building, or they may be coordinated programs. The library program may be located in a single reading room the size of one or two classrooms, in a suite of rooms on one or two floors, or in separate reading rooms scattered throughout the school plant. The library suite may be located either in the administrative or in the teaching area. In some schools, subject reading rooms and resources learning centers may be located in different parts of the school plant or campus, near the academic departments they serve. In one large suburban school with an enrollment of several thousand students, the one-building school is divided into four "schools within a school" each with separate administrative and teaching staffs; each with its own quarters for library service.

Consultant and Supervisory Services

Along with the consolidation and reorganization of local schools, consultant and supervisory services have been strengthened and developed at the state, county, city, and local levels. One significant reason for this has been the gradual shift in the last 30 years from local financial support of elementary and secondary schools to financing of special projects through state and federal grants. Well-designed educational programs take time and leadership to develop and to operate. Therefore, only schools developing experimental projects to improve their present instructional programs request such funds. State aid is given also to schools that are unable to support their regular school programs but desire to meet state and regional standards. Curriculum consultants and media specialists have been added to local administrative staffs to improve teaching methods, to provide for needed instructional materials, and to plan experiments for developing quality programs of instruction. Since grants from federal sources are given only upon evidence of good state planning with guidelines for administering federal funds to insure wise use of the money, the consultant staff at the state level has also been increased to administer such programs. Many of these consultants have played a significant role in developing experimental programs in teaching. These programs, in turn, have affected the development and improvement of school library services.

Experimental teaching programs such as team teaching, ungraded classes, individualized reading, large and small group instruction, and special classes for able students and for culturally disadvantaged children, have led many teachers and subject specialists to recognize the need for resources of all types to enrich the learning process. The development of educational uses of media such as television, programmed learning, teaching machines, and electronic learning devices has emphasized the role of school libraries as centers of learning, because they make available book and nonbook resources to meet the local needs of children and youth. Teachers are becoming aware of the importance of using library materials, especially when they prepare programmed instruction or large-group lectures. Students also use a variety of materials to supplement and to clarify what they have seen or heard, as well as for independent study projects.

Libraries in schools are not new nor are library consultants at state and local levels, but libraries have been changing as teaching methods have been changing to meet the challenges of the modern school. States and local school systems that have provided directors or consultants for school libraries and teaching materials have progressed rapidly in planning and developing library programs of service that provide for the total instructional needs of pupils and teachers.

District Instructional Media Centers

With nonprint resources and programmed television instruction being used in many schools, the cost of instructional materials has been prohibitive for most individual schools. Planned uses of television by large groups, scheduled uses of expensive films, and cooperative planning for use of museum objects and realia have led to the development of district instructional media centers where all teaching materials can be centrally purchased and processed.

At the county or system level, the services of the district IMC follow a general pattern, with variations depending upon the length of time the center has been in operation, the size of the staff, the number of schools being serviced, and its administrative organization. The smaller the system and the more recent its development, the more the administration of the center is apt to be under the direction of a school library specialist. Large metropolitan centers have highly specialized personnel and separate divisions for various types of materials and services which are coordinated by an administrative officer.

Administration of the District Instructional Media Center

District IMC's have no set pattern of administrative organization. In some systems the administrative head may be called the Director of the Division of Instructional Materials, the Director of Learning Resources, or the Director of Educational Media. Such officials come from the administrative staff of the school system. Under their administrator, the division specialists coordinate the library program, the audiovisual program, the professional library, the curriculum laboratory, and the textbook program. District centers provide supplementary production services for the teaching staff including illustrating, mounting, lettering, coloring, photography, and the preparation of more elaborate transparencies for use with the overhead projector than are usually produced in a local school library. Centralized purchasing and processing of library materials—book and nonbook—for each school library in the system may be provided. Periodically, statistics on the increasing number of school districts providing centralized processing of library materials have been available from the U.S. Office of Education. District centers may also provide in-service training programs to assist teachers to effectively use new media as it becomes available from the district center.

In some district centers the school library specialist serves as the director of library services and the coordinator of instructional materials of the center in addition to supervising the library programs at the school level. This is the pattern in Houston, Texas; Webster Parish, Minden, Louisiana; and Skokie, Illinois. An increasing number of such assignments are being made because the school library specialist is prepared to understand curriculum development; to select, to evaluate, and to assist in the use of all types of materials in relation to the reading and informational needs and abilities of students; and to plan for the organization of these materials for effective use by pupils and teachers. Staff members of the district center include persons with technical background in production techniques, in processing of materials for use, and in the installation and supervision of electronic equipment and machines.

Other school systems have selected the audiovisual specialist to coordinate the instructional media program and the processing services at the district IMC and to supervise the library program in each school. This is the pattern in a few school districts in Arizona, California, Florida, Illinois, and Indiana; however, examples do not reflect a dominant trend.

Still another administrative pattern of the district IMC is to divide the responsibility by having two administrative staff members: a school library supervisor responsible for the professional library, for central processing, and for coordinating library services in each school; and an audiovisual specialist responsible for all nonbook materials and for the distribution of these resources to teachers in each school. The audiovisual specialist usually works with a liaison teacher or school principal in each school to coordinate requests for nonbook materials to be delivered daily or weekly to the schools.

The services provided by a school district IMC vary as widely as the administrative organization. In some school systems all nonprint materials are centrally administered from the district IMC and go directly to the classroom teacher. Films, filmstrips, tapes, recordings, slides, resources kits, museum objects, and pictures are listed in printed catalogs that are distributed to each classroom teacher. Subject and grade level approaches are usually described in the catalogs.

Although these holdings are not generally included in the school library card catalog, the printed catalog is available in the library. Where materials are being centrally processed, the trend is to include all types of teaching materials and to file cards for nonbook materials in the card catalog of the school library.

In school systems where all nonprint resources are centrally housed in and serviced from the district IMC, rather than from the local school library, such resources are intended primarily for use by teachers in the classrooms. The school library and/or classroom collections contain only the printed resources such as books, pamphlets, newspapers, and magazines for use by pupils and teachers. Student use of nonbook materials is thus limited to the classroom and is usually teacher directed. In contrast, resources located in the school library are used by pupils as well as by teachers. Scheduled daily, biweekly, or weekly deliveries from the district center bring these non-print materials to teachers requesting them. Request forms are provided for teachers, and advanced bookings give assurance that materials will be available when needed. Some school systems have sufficient resources and clerical staff to make possible daily telephone service for additional requests for teaching materials. Broward County, Florida, has just introduced an electronic data processing booking system to facilitate circulation.

Centralization of audiovisual resources at the district IMC is found in school systems having few or no elementary school libraries, an inadequate library staff, or very limited resources in classroom collections. Centralization of media at the district center is also frequent when the supervisor of school libraries is an audiovisual specialist rather than a school library specialist.

A more recent and rapidly developing trend is toward the decentralization of most nonprint resources from the district center to the individual school. More effective use can be made of filmstrips, recordings, and taped materials when these resources and equipment are available to pupils and teachers in a school library. Handviewers and listening posts in school libraries, in study areas, and in classrooms make it possible for children and young people to use these learning materials for independent study whenever they are needed, just as they use books and magazines. They are also readily available for large or small group use in the classroom.

The district IMC keeps the expensive items such as films, museum objects, resources kits, and other nonbook materials that are less frequently requested but occasionally needed for teacher or classroom use. Usually, the district IMC provides each school with catalogs of resources to be found at the district center and catalog cards showing those resources located in the school. Practices will depend upon the stage of development of centralized or data processing of instructional materials. For example, in Greensboro, North Carolina, all types of materials are centrally processed at the district IMC and cards for each media are filed in each school library.

The district IMC thus provides supplementary services and resources for the schools in the system. Some types of materials such as filmstrips, resources kits, and recordings are found both at the district IMC and in a central school library. But the major services offered by the district center include (1) a professional library, (2) sophisticated and expensive production services to supplement those found in the school library, (3) in-service education, (4) central purchasing and processing of instructional materials, (5) an audiovisual program to make available expensive nonbook resources, and (6) studios for closed circuit educational television and radio programs oriented to the curriculum needs of the system. A wealth of resources or a paucity of materials is found in varying degrees in most states.

Cooperative Film Centers

Many school systems do not operate a district IMC and do not have supplementary resources to send to their schools; other systems provide only a few professional books and a few films to supplement school-owned books. Many independent and parochial schools do not have access to a district center. Sometimes the schools in a county or school unit area find it expedient to work out cooperative plans for securing selected educational films for use by member schools. Cook and DuPage counties in Illinois have centers that work out of the county superintendent's office and serve public, parochial, and private elementary and high schools in the area. Assessments are based on a formula including enrollment, the number of delivery stops per year, and cost of boxes to carry films. Many schools own their own delivery boxes. Title catalogs and subject lists are made available to member schools and some NDEA monies are used to purchase film titles or science models for member schools. These centers often provide a curriculum library and a professional library for teachers. The curriculum guides and latest samples of texts are usually noncirculating, while science curriculum materials and professional literature relating to the gifted child, the culturally disadvantaged, and slow learners are loaned to schools or to individual teachers. The types of resources, the selection of titles, and services vary greatly and depend upon the needs of the member schools, the amount of money available, the size of staff, and headquarters space.

Inter-School Projects

Communities in the beginning stages of developing library services in elementary schools or communities in which the only professional librarian is in the high school, sometimes coordinate all nonbook resources in the high school library. These filmstrips, recordings, slides, and films are then shared with the elementary schools of the system. Simple procedures are set up and mimeographed lists are distributed to teachers in the system informing them of the titles available. Active PTA groups often contribute money to purchase the audiovisual equipment for each building. Efforts of this nature depend upon the willingness of the school librarian to extend and expand the library resources for use in other schools of the system. From such small beginnings have developed planned programs of library service for all schools.

Implications of Federal Legislation

Federal legislation to provide funds for supplementing instructional materials in schools sets forth recommendations for regional and cooperative centers to supplement book and nonbook materials and services for children and youth in public, parochial, and private schools. Wise planning can enrich the resources now available and provide books, films, recordings, filmstrips, and other nonbook materials to schools that have none of these resources. For example, a regional instructional materials and processing center could provide:

1. educational radio and television production and broadcasting facilities;
2. centralized processing of all library materials for all schools in the region for a small charge per item;

3. a large and comprehensive film library;

4. a filmstrip library to supplement the collection in small or new schools, and to enrich instruction in all schools;

5. phonograph records, tapes, transcriptions, study prints, models, realia, and other audiovisual materials;

6. a professional library for teachers providing books, pamphlets, curriculum guides, sample textbooks and workbooks, multiple copies of textbooks to supplement classroom texts, if needed, and other materials;

7. educational consultants for art, science, social studies, vocational education, and special programs for the gifted and for the culturally deprived;

8. a research center that could utilize the professional staffs and resources of the universities in the area;

9. a production center to provide supplementary teaching aids for teachers.

The center described would be a natural repository for the expensive materials to be purchased under Title III of the Elementary and Secondary Education Act of 1965, and such materials could be loaned to public and nonprofit private schools, including the parochial schools.

Administrative Patterns in School Libraries

In traditional schools the school library resources and programs of service are primarily book centered. The collections include magazines, newspapers, pamphlets, and a few pictures as well as the books which are organized for use by pupils and teachers. Nonbook materials and the equipment to project and record them are not provided by the library. If any nonbook resources are school-owned, they are usually located in classrooms, in departmental offices, in laboratories, or even in the principal's office. No effort is made by the librarian to catalog these nonbook materials, and they will be used in classroom situations only if teachers happen to be aware that they exist in the school. Materials ordered by previous teachers usually remain in cupboards, unused and unknown to other faculty members.

Films that are needed for classroom use are usually ordered through the school office. In some schools a teacher who is capable of running motion picture projectors is assigned to handle the audiovisual equipment and also serves as a building coordinator for the ordering of films and other audiovisual resources requested by the classroom teacher. Disc recordings are usually in the music department and in physical education offices for use in dance and rhythm classes. Seldom is any effort made to organize them for use outside the classroom.

Some schools still order films to be viewed by the entire school. Pupils are brought to the assembly hall or to the gym to see a film, regardless of whether it fits into a class unit. Nonstructured use of audiovisual materials is most common when communities lack school libraries of any type and when teaching methods are textbook centered.

Teacher-librarians who have only a few hours a day or week to work in a library find it difficult to organize for use even the book resources of the school. Larger schools employ full-time librarians but often no clerical staff to handle the technical details of library administration. Since much of the servicing of nonbook materials is of a technical and clerical nature, many school librarians are reluctant to undertake this additional phase of instructional resources unless sufficient staff is provided to handle the program.

The Audiovisual Department in a School

In the past 30 years, use of nonbook materials such as films, filmstrips, slides, recordings, and transparencies has increased in almost every department of the school and at all grade levels. When the school librarian was reluctant or refused to service nonbook materials needed in the classroom, many larger schools employed an audiovisual specialist. As the program developed, a separate audiovisual department was often organized to provide special services, including:

1. maintaining audiovisual equipment;
2. training student projectionists;
3. scheduling and ordering free and rental films for classroom use;
4. purchasing and organizing nonbook materials such as filmstrips, tapes, recordings, maps, realia, and slides;
5. producing teaching materials such as transparencies, slides, tapes, and posters;

6. publishing mimeographed or printed catalogs of nonbook materials;

7. compiling subject and grade level indexes of nonbook resources.

The extent of the resources available to the school depends upon whether the school is independent or part of a school system that has a district or system center to supplement its holdings. The audiovisual specialist usually works closely with teachers to plan for the effective use of nonbook teaching resources. The extent of teacher planning depends upon the philosophy and preparation of the audiovisual specialist. The professional preparation of the audiovisual specialist emphasizes curriculum development and organization of materials for effective use. In schools with educational television and radio programs, language laboratories, electronic learning centers, and production centers, the audiovisual department is responsible for installation and maintenance of this equipment.

Often the library and the audiovisual departments give very little evidence of a close working relationship. Each goes its separate way and provides independent services for teachers. In this case nonbook materials are used mostly by teachers in classroom situations and are seldom available for student use. Teachers who wish to use all types of materials in a teaching unit have to search for materials in more than one place; they must look in a card catalog and in a printed catalog, even though the two departments may be located next to each other.

Coordinated Library and Audiovisual Departments

Programs and services between the library and the audiovisual departments can be coordinated at the building level. The book and nonbook materials and the services appropriate to each are administered in separate departments, but the working relationship of the two divisions is planned as a unit to provide maximum service to teachers and students. Such programs are usually called instructional media centers and include library specialists and audiovisual specialists administering each type of program. The new media standards indicate the type of specialists needed for such a program.

When the departments are separate but coordinated, the nonbook materials and equipment are located in the audiovisual wing or area of the IMC. Purchasing films, renting them, and scheduling them for classroom or school use, production services, and the other types of service suggested above are the responsibility of the audiovisual department. The professional preparation of the librarian and of the audiovisual specialist may be different, but both should have an understanding of curriculum needs and both should work closely with each other and with the faculty in helping to plan units of study. Student use as well as classroom use of book and nonprint materials can be encouraged because listening posts, viewing areas, and handviewers are provided in the IMC. Darkroom facilities, production areas, and studios for closed circuit television are sometimes included if funds and space permit. These services will be less inclusive if services are available from a district IMC. Good working relationships are often dependent upon the personalities of the individuals themselves and upon their philosophies of service.

In coordinated programs, the different types of nonbook materials as well as all printed materials are included in the card catalog. Cards for materials may be differentiated by means of cards of various colors, color-banded white cards, or a symbol next to the call number to designate a film, filmstrip, recording, transparency, or any other type of nonbook material. Such a catalog includes referral cards for supplementary materials in the vertical file, in picture files, in classroom collections, in laboratories, or in other libraries in the community. All school-owned instructional materials are indexed in the card catalog regardless of their location so that pupils and teachers can locate many kinds of resources by looking in only one source.

Study of the Library as a Media Center

A general current trend is the changing role of the school library from a book-centered program to that of a media-centered program of services and resources. Many school libraries have been moving in this direction for years. As newer materials of instruction were produced for classrooms, school librarians purchased and organized them. Experiments were undertaken in the organization of these media for use by students and teachers, and standard patterns were developed for arranging films, recordings, slides, and tapes for use in a school library.

Efforts are still being made throughout the country to implement the school library standards of 1945 [1] and 1960 [2] and to build up an understanding of the philosophy of service expressed by the national standards. The new standards, published in the spring of 1969, spell them out in more detail, in sections dealing with (1) staff and services, (2) selection, accessibility, and organization of materials, (3) size and budget; (4) facilities, and (5) supplemental services. [3]

In order to determine whether school libraries were accepting the role of the library as a media center, a status study to identify such school libraries was undertaken during 1962 and 1963. This study was authorized by the U.S. Office of Education, Educational Media Branch of Section 731, Part B of Title VII of Public Law 85–864. As the study progressed one fact was evident: Many elementary, junior high, and senior high schools have library programs functioning as instructional media centers. These are located in all parts of the United States, in small and in large schools, and in all types of communities. In 30 states 411 school library programs were identified and 203 of them were observed in varied types of schools, some with enrollments of less than 200 and some with more than 4,000.

Not all school libraries had rich resources of book and nonbook materials, nor adequate quarters, equipment, budget, or staff to develop programs to meet the recommendations of the national standards. Many were in the beginning stages of developing such programs and resources, but what was available represented the broader concept of a media centered program. There were, however, 41 school libraries in 17 states that had outstanding resources and programs of library services. Undoubtedly, many others that were not identified or that have been built since the study would also rank in the top group of school libraries. Of the schools identified, almost half met the national standards for holdings of books, magazines, newspapers, and audiovisual materials. Good book collections were usually accompanied by good resources of vertical file, professional, and audiovisual materials. Good collections of instructional materials were often associated with dynamic library programs of services, good reading programs, individualized instruction, advanced placement at the high school level, emphasis on academic programs, flexible library scheduling of pupils in the elementary schools, use of educational television and radio, language laboratories, and reading laboratories with teaching machines.

The best libraries had good financial support. The weakest link in the chain was professional and clerical staff adequate to give individualized service to pupils and teachers. Yet many of the schools had clerical and professional staffs, the latter with special subject backgrounds and with audiovisual preparation and experience.

Schools having abundant instructional resources were not limited to any geographical area, type of school, or type of community. Many had participated in national studies and research projects. A fairly large proportion of the graduates of the high schools were college bound. Even when the student body was average, with few if any gifted students, the students were good readers and had access to many types of instructional materials selected to meet their individual learning needs. Students went to the library to do independent research and pleasure reading. They went in classes, in small groups, or as individuals. Reading was at the core of this kind of program, but all types of materials were used to make reading experiences more meaningful. The IMCs served to challenge the student, to enrich the curriculum, and to provide for recreational reading, listening, or viewing activities.

Organization of Materials and Services of the IMC

Many of the smaller instructional media centers have only one reading room with a combination office, workroom, and storage area. The materials, however, are organized as a unit. Special book and nonbook materials that are continuously used in a music or shop program may be housed in those departments on permanent loans. Classes, groups, or individuals may also come to the IMC as the need arises to use the resources for preparing reports, papers, class projects, or individual pursuits.

The location of nonbook materials usually depends upon whether the library was designed as a materials center or was remodeled into one. Filmstrips, recordings, tapes, and models, even when housed in the workroom and storage area, are usually available for use by students and teachers. Small handviewers, listening stations, and individual carrels, with or without electrical outlets, are in the reading room.

Whether the recordings and filmstrips are housed in the IMC along with the books or in separate cabinets depends upon the space available. In some IMCs, shelves have been specially designed to house nonbook materials along with the printed materials. In others, special cabinets and cupboards house these media. The classification arrangements are also dependent upon space facilities. If filmstrips, for example, are stored in small cans that must be fitted into special slots, the classification is usually a location number. Many subject entries and cross references are needed to locate an item. On the other hand, if the equipment for filmstrips is designed for flexible storage, filmstrips can be classified in the same manner as books. Just as new books are intershelved, so filmstrips are interfiled in drawers or shelves or cabinets with those previously purchased. Public shelf lists with all types of materials classified and interfiled simplify the task of compiling bibliographies of materials. The card catalog also has cards for materials of each type arranged alphabetically in a dictionary catalog, or arranged in separate author and subject catalogs.

Even small IMCs provide production areas and services for students and teachers to make their own materials such as transparencies and other illustrative materials. Pupil assistants plan and make exhibits and design bulletin board displays. The production area is also used for the mechanical preparation and mending of books. Few small schools provide darkroom facilities, but if there is a district IMC for the schools one is usually provided there. The production area in the average school is for the simpler and less elaborate equipment needed for illustrating class projects.

Larger schools and recently designed schools have the same basic pattern for organizing materials for use, but they may have satellite learning centers and service areas available as part of the instructional media center. The typical suite of rooms includes (1) a general browsing and reading room, (2) three or four subject-area rooms, (3) offices, (4) storage areas, (5) production areas, (6) a professional library for teachers, and (7) studios for radio and television.

In addition to the suite of rooms, adjacent study areas under the supervision of teachers or teacher aides may have resources supplied by the library for units of study in language arts, science, or social studies. Learning resources centers scattered throughout the school plant may also be under the supervision of teacher aides with instructional materials supplied from the main library. Such resources centers may be a part of the language laboratory complex, the reading laboratory, and/or the science and mathematics departments. Many schools engaged in modern teaching programs, finding it hard to justify traditional study halls, develop learning resources centers instead. A single textbook is inadequate for the needs of individual students and cannot adequately cover the content of modern courses. Large-group instruction and individualized study programs require more modern approaches to instructional resources.

Naturally, each department of the school has its special supplementary classroom materials. But no matter where these are located, the IMC maintains a record of all school-owned holdings. Simple records are kept, but the media center assumes responsibility for recording all items in its indexes. In this manner no department or classroom teacher is deprived of convenient access to often-used teaching materials, but they are likewise available to other teachers and to students. Efficient organization, elimination of expensive duplication, and guidance in the utilization of all types of learning materials result.

Conclusions

Just as there is no one pattern of school organization in the United States, so there is no one pattern of organizing instructional materials for most efficient use. Each school develops its own educational philosophy in terms of community needs, of teaching methods used, and of the needs of the boys and girls in that school. Each school board is responsible for financing the teaching program developed by its school officials and its teaching faculty. The library program and the instructional materials that supplement the teaching program reflect the philosophy of the school, the teaching methods of the faculty, and the support given by the school administration and the school board. Therefore, many and varied patterns of organization are found in school libraries. Some libraries are traditionally book oriented; others have developed a program of service to make all types of instructional materials available to students and teachers for class and for independent study. Some schools have no library service at all.

Although the professional preparation of the teaching and the library staffs, the attitude of the library staff toward nonbook materials, and the size of the library staff all play a part in determining the pattern of organization for the school library, there is much evidence that the current trend is in the direction of developing the school library as an instructional media center of service. More and more states are employing state and local school library supervisors to develop instructional media centers. National and state standards reflect this philosophy, and dynamic programs of library services functioning as instructional media centers have been identified in more than 30 states.

Research in the psychology of learning and in communication media shows that each child is unique in his capacity to learn, in his rate of learning, in his personal needs and interests, and in the effective use he makes of the media of communication in the learning process. School libraries that select, organize for use, and encourage the use of all types of instructional materials are able to care for the individual differences of each student. These libraries are found in small schools as well as in large ones. Librarians and teachers in these schools are partners in planning, developing, and implementing the kind of teaching program that will produce quality education. The patterns of organization are dynamic and changing, tailored to meet the teaching and learning needs of faculty and students. The relevant library must function as an instructional media center.

CHAPTER 5

Organizing an IMC

by

Harold S. Davis

Harold S. Davis is a professor of education and chairman of the Educational Administration and Supervision Department, Southern Connecticut State College. Prior to accepting his present position, he was director of in-service education and staff utilization for the Educational Research Council of America where he was responsible for training administrators and teachers in 30 school districts. In addition, he has served as special consultant to more than 100 school systems and universities throughout the United States.

Dr. Davis has more than 20 years experience as a teacher, counselor, administrator, and educational consultant. He holds a graduate degree in mathematics and a doctorate in school administration from Wayne State University. He has also studied in England at Oxford University and in France at the University of Paris. He is the author of the book How to Organize an Effective Team Teaching Program *as well as numerous pamphlets and articles on modern approaches to education.*

THOMAS JEFFERSON ONCE SAID: "As new discoveries are made, new truths discovered and manners and opinions change, with the change of circumstances, institutions must advance also to keep pace with the times." These are such times, and educators are now beginning to realize they can no longer use methods of the past to prepare for the future. Children who are taught to memorize and repeat are not adequately prepared to think and create. We must place our emphasis on comprehension rather than regurgitation, on research rather than rote.

In the midst of a technological revolution, too many schools are still committed to a creeping evolution. Ignoring mass media and machines, old-fashioned teachers restrict their pupils to rooms containing only blackboards and books. By contrast, modern educators are establishing instructional media centers that encourage exploration and discovery. They surround the pupil with every form of expression known to man: materials to stimulate his eye, his ear, his mind. In developing such IMCs, three patterns of organization have emerged: (1) the centralized IMC; (2) the decentralized IMC; and (3) the coordinated IMC.

The Centralized IMC

A centralized IMC is one that functions as the sole facility within a school district responsible for acquiring, cataloging, and storing instructional materials. Usually, such a facility is available to teachers only and not to students. Obviously, the value of the center is linked to the effectiveness of its distribution plan. Materials such as films, filmstrips, and recordings have little value for teachers if they arrive late. Their real worth is derived from being integrated into a specific lesson.

A centralized IMC is generally the least expensive type to operate because it requires no duplication of space, equipment, or staff. Disorganized building collections may be consolidated into a single organized collection which can give teachers access to all available materials. Such a system minimizes problems of loose accounting and inadequate storage. A centralized IMC provides the first step toward modernization for any school system lacking school libraries. In contrast to decentralized libraries, which require a librarian in each building, the centralized IMC may be operated by one librarian reinforced with clerical help. Savings on staff alone are often decisive in determining the organizational pattern.

Although the centralized IMC is relatively inexpensive and efficient, it becomes increasingly difficult to operate as a school system expands. Demands of a growing teaching staff require constant increases in both book and nonbook collections. With expansion, catalogs must be kept current to meet needs and to facilitate distribution of materials. A coordinator is usually appointed in each building to consolidate teacher requests. At this point, centralized IMCs often make semipermanent loans to individual schools and thus shift toward decentralization.

The Decentralized IMC

A decentralized IMC is one which functions as an independent facility within a given school building. It is responsible for acquiring, cataloging, and storing instructional materials. Generally, such an IMC is available for use by students as well as teachers and is designed to serve the needs of the single school in which it is located. Such a facility is usually an outgrowth of a school library and is based upon the concept that teachers will make the greatest use of materials that are readily available. Many teachers prepare their own transparencies and tapes and find such media more valuable in instruction than their commercial counterparts.

In a study conducted by Indiana University for the U.S. Office of Education (Circular 718, U.S. Department of Health, Education, and Welfare, 1963) more than 75 percent of the teachers stated they had benefited from producing their own instructional materials. A majority would prefer making their own materials "if time was allocated during the regular school day for this activity." They concluded that when teachers are given "the time and encouragement to improve their classroom presentations, they tend to begin searching for better ways to visualize the ideas and concepts they want students to understand."

However, pupils also need ready access to the IMC. They learn from a variety of sources, both audio and visual. Books, alone, are not enough. Students enjoy learning from the newer media and should be encouraged to use visual materials in the preparation and presentation of their own classroom reports. Certainly, any student engaged in research should have ready access to all the materials he needs.

Teaching machines and programmed learning materials also warrant a place and space in the IMC. Although their value has not been clearly established, the methodology is improving. For example, a two-year study at the University of South Florida showed that retarded children learned to read faster and more effectively by means of teaching machines than by attending conventional reading classes.

Experiments with I.P.I. (individually prescribed instruction) and other programmed learning materials also show great promise.

Terminals for computer-assisted instruction are no longer a novelty and may become conventional items in future IMCs. Talking typewriters and the new talking page, which are proving their value as autotutorial devices, should be considered when media purchases are being made.

Because decentralization puts materials closer to the user, the process has been carried one step farther in some schools through the development of departmental learning centers. For example, a large school may contain separate centers for mathematics, science, English, or social science as satellites of the school IMC. However, these centers should not be confused with traditional classroom libraries. Pupils have access to a complete range of materials and are not limited to an inadequate collection maintained by a classroom teacher. In any school IMC, students learn to use the card catalog, reference books, slides, tapes, filmstrips, and records. The entire collection of book and nonbook materials is available for use by a maximum number of pupils. Even primary teachers find that a school IMC provides greater enjoyment to children as they explore more books and materials than ever before. In a properly equipped IMC, pupils have a place to read, write, view, think, and discuss.

To care for the needs of teachers who desire classroom materials, school IMCs should maintain a book-truck service. Working with the teacher, the librarian may assemble the needed materials and have them delivered to classrooms on mobile carts. After the materials have been used and are no longer needed, they are returned to the central collection for use by others. In this way the building IMC provides an efficient, effective, schoolwide educational service.

The Coordinated IMC

A coordinated instructional media center operates as a system. It contains a network of school IMCs linked to a central IMC. It is a natural evolution in any district where education rather than cost is foremost in planning. In a coordinated system, each school develops its own IMC, but is supplemented and served by a district center which provides additional equipment and service. Equipment that each school cannot afford or would seldom use, is kept in the district IMC.

For example, the film library is maintained at the district level while the projectors are available at the individual school. Similarly, expensive TV studio equipment is maintained at the district IMC, while less expensive videotape players are on hand in the school. Cumbersome opaque projectors are available at the district level, while more versatile overhead projectors are supplied to each building. A costly microfilm reader-printer is part of every district IMC, while the inexpensive microfilm reader should be available in every school. In this way, the district center coordinates the operation of the entire system and serves as a supplement to each of the building IMCs.

Designing the IMC

The IMC should be designed for the users, not the librarian. In traditional school libraries, pupils are herded together in the middle of a large room, seated face to face around tables (a perfect psychological setting for discussion), and are then ordered to be silent. Every comment, every dropped pencil or book, every trip to the bookshelves, is a distraction to all. No wonder so many librarians, driven to the point of desperation, resort to authoritarian tactics. If present procedures were reversed and free standing bookshelves were placed about the room, with study carrels along the walls, students could move to the shelves without disturbing others. By grouping bookcases into various patterns, large rooms can be broken up into smaller, more intimate study areas.

According to Ralph Ellsworth, a leading consultant on library construction, "It has been proven over and over again in college libraries that students don't like to read in large, open reading rooms. They like the privacy and the intimacy of small groups. They do not want to sit at flat tables in the middle of a large reading room." This attitude is expressed also by elementary and secondary school pupils, who have enthusiastically accepted the introduction of study carrels.

Free standing carrels, in addition to wall carrels and occasional tables, help soften the pattern. Acoustical floor covering (commercial carpeting) prevents noise before it begins and makes more sense than trapping noise in the ceiling after it has proven a distraction. As a result, carpeted, air-conditioned IMCs, once considered a luxury, are now becoming more common. Not only do such facilities provide year-round comfort, but they produce savings when architects are allowed to depart from traditional patterns to provide more compact, air-conditioned school plants.

A concern for individuality is evident in many IMCs. Attention has been given to providing comfortable, attractive furniture. Manufacturers admit that much library furniture is uncomfortable and poorly designed. Behavior problems often fade when IMCs are designed for the ease and convenience of the pupil and decorated to elicit his pride and respect. As Goethe said: "If you treat an individual as he is, he will stay as he is, but if you treat him as if he were what he ought to be and could be, he will become what he ought to be and could be."

Space and location also must be considered. While most studies indicate that an IMC should seat 15 to 30 percent of the student body at one time, many schools still construct libraries with room for less than 10 percent of their enrollment. Obviously, they are not looking ahead to the day when increasing amounts of time will be spent in independent study activities.

If we are to truly individualize learning, independent study must become a regularly scheduled part of the instructional program. This should not be confused with "homework." At home, pupils often are limited to a library consisting of the textbook; brothers, sisters, or pets interfere with study; the stereo or TV prevents concentration; and no one is available as a resource except mom or dad. Independent study should place an emphasis on creative, meaningful research that stretches and strengthens the mind of each student. Such research requires facilities and materials conducive to study. Pupils engaged in independent study need study carrels for reading, writing, and typing. They need stations for viewing and listening. They need to see films and filmstrips, to hear tapes and records. They need space for committee work and group projects.

In such an environment, students learn effective work-study skills and a sense of individual responsibility. It is essential that such facilities be located where teachers and pupils will use them to the maximum. However, if an IMC is placed in the geometric center of the school, it may be inconvenient for evening or weekend use. Preferably, the IMC should be on the ground floor near exits and parking. Students needing access to books, pamphlets, and magazines or to tapes and filmstrips should not be denied access to these materials outside the normal school day. Many would appreciate the opportunity to use a modern IMC for research and other projects. We must be prepared to replace "keep out" signs with "welcome" mats! As service becomes a keynote, usage will increase. Therefore, the IMC design should allow for future expansion as additional space is needed.

Poorly ventilated, dimly lit, badly furnished libraries of the past were designed for the past. They were apart from, not a part of, the curriculum. They were mere storehouses for materials unneeded in the classroom. Now that modern librarians and architects have shown that libraries can be simultaneously practical and pleasing, all educators should take a careful look at aesthetic possibilities in school plant planning.

Resistance to Change

Resistance to change is almost an instinct. Egyptian librarians complained about the change from sturdy stone and clay tablets to flimsy papyrus scrolls. In the fifteenth century, librarians argued against adding printed books to their collections of handwritten documents. Such books were considered ugly and undignified.

Today, some librarians resent, resist, or refuse to extend their responsibilities to the handling of nonbook materials. Their negative attitudes impede progress and thwart the process of correlating audiovisual and library functions. Librarians must expand their professional roles or relinquish their tasks to others. Some wonder why resistance to change is so prevelant. Perhaps Woodrow Wilson had the answer. In July, 1916, while addressing a conference in Detroit, he said: "If you want to make enemies, try to change something. You know why it is. To do things today exactly the way you did them yesterday saves thinking. It does not cost you anything. You have acquired the habit; you know the routine; you do not have to plan anything, and it frightens you with a hint of exertion to learn that you will have to do it a different way tomorrow." This stance was typified by a librarian who was retiring after 40 years of service. When asked if she had seen many changes in her long career, she replied: "Yes, and I've been against every one of them."

Not all librarians are that obdurate. Many observers believe the real blame for lack of progress can be placed on a penurious public. According to the July 1962 issue of *Overview*, "75 percent of our elementary schools and nearly 60 percent of our high schools do not have library facilities." U.S. Department of Health, Education, and

Welfare Office of Education figures published in 1964 were more favorable, but still showed 51.7 percent of all schools lacked libraries. Further, many so-called "libraries" are small rooms containing only a collection of old novels and outdated encyclopedias. Most of these dismal places inhibit rather than stimulate learning. In fact, Report No. 1 of the Deiches Fund Studies of Public Library Services, *Students and the Pratt Library: Challenge and Opportunity,* shows that approximately three-fourths of the student readers prefer using public libraries rather than school libraries because of more adequate collections, more suitable hours of service, and fewer restrictions and controls.

Excessive restrictions and controls are unfortunate holdovers from the past. In the Middle Ages, libraries discouraged book borrowing, often chained books to the walls, and customarily barred readers from the stacks. Some librarians still see themselves as book custodians rather than circulation builders. This attitude can best be illustrated by the following anecdote once recounted by Charles Eliot Norton of Harvard. Norton met the librarian on the campus one day and asked how things were going. "Excellently, excellently," said the librarian. "All the books are on the shelves except the one Agassiz has, and I'm going after that now."

Recommendations for Change

Fortunately a growing number of librarians are turning their backs upon the past and looking forward to the future. As far back as 1960, the American Association of School Librarians in *Standards for School Library Programs* stated: "The American Association of School Librarians believes that the school library, in addition to doing its vital work of individual reading guidance and development of the school curriculum, should serve the school as a center for instructional materials. Instructional materials include books—the literature of children, young people and adults—other printed materials, films, recordings, and newer media developed to aid learning."

In its *Policies and Criteria for the Approval of Secondary Schools,* The North Central Association of College and Secondary Schools tells applicants for accreditation: "The library shall be organized as a resource center of instructional materials for the entire educational program. The number and kind of library and reference books, periodicals, newspapers, pamphlets, information files, audiovisual materials, and other learning aids shall be adequate for the number of pupils and the needs of instruction in all courses." The weakness of this recommendation lies in the words "shall be adequate." Inspection teams, often composed of quite conservative administrators, usually find the traditional library to be an "adequate" IMC.

The NEA also added support for the establishment of IMCs in its report *Schools for the Sixties*. Recommendation number 28 states: "In each school system, there should be one or more well-planned instructional materials and resources centers, consisting of at least a library and an audiovisual center. In each school building, there should also be an instructional resources facility. . . . These centers should be staffed with persons who are adequately prepared in curriculum and instruction, in library service, and in audiovisual education." [1] The project committee felt that, "each school ought to have an instructional resources center containing library books and instructional materials that are most constantly in use, plus information on resources which are available elsewhere."

As a result of these and other recommendations, many new IMCs have been established. But the mere establishment of an IMC does not guarantee that it will function as intended. There are poor IMCs just as there are poor libraries. Members of the Graduate School of Library Science, University of Illinois, visited representative American IMCs in 1961 and found many to be quite traditional. Alice Lohrer, an inspection team member, reported that in some cases "the library and the audiovisual departments were completely separated and lacked coordination." She stated: "Resistance to coordination was expressed in terms of lack of professional staff, lack of professional preparation, lack of space, lack of equipment, lack of money for books alone, and lack of interest." Obviously, the establishment of an IMC must be accompanied by an intensive in-service education program for teachers and principals as well as librarians. All need to familiarize themselves with the functions of an IMC if they and their pupils are to make effective use of the facility.

Recognition of Change

Fortunately, an ever-increasing number of school districts are blessed with dedicated boards of education and service-minded librarians.

Educators are becoming aware of the fact that when they establish a climate designed to stimulate thinking, the odds are that such thinking will take place. As a result, a rich variety of materials, facilities, and equipment is being offered to teachers and pupils to help them reach their educational goals. A new spirit of academic enterprise is replacing old prejudices and complacent rigidities.

With a growing emphasis upon individualized instruction, modern librarians are removing traditional restrictions to make the IMC an inviting, lively place in which to learn. They are helping students develop responsibility and self-direction. They are making independent study a major educational objective. They are encouraging a more flexible use of time, space, and materials. They are engaging in teamwork with teachers and are promoting a shift from teaching by telling to learning by doing.

A Centralized IMC in Action

Harkness Center, Buffalo, New York, provides an excellent example of how districts can combine their resources to provide service no district could supply alone. Eighteen school districts, serving approximately 4,000 teachers in over 100 schools formed the instructional materials and teacher training center known as Harkness Center.

This program was an outgrowth of several other cooperative programs conducted by these districts in conjunction with the Board of Cooperative Educational Services (BOCES) of the First Supervisory District in Erie County, New York. The BOCES, a legally constituted educational agency of the state, was organized to encourage school districts to cooperatively sponsor programs they could not afford to operate alone.

Through centralization, even the smallest of the 18 districts has access to videotapes, films, equipment and training facilities normally found only in large or wealthy school systems. For example, all teachers are provided with a film catalog listing over 4,000 prints. Any print is available upon request and is delivered to and picked up at the individual school. Although requests for films and projectors normally are submitted a week or more in advance of delivery, orders can be filled more rapidly if necessary.

A library of curriculum guides, donated by participating schools, is also in the IMC along with curriculum improvement materials of modern programs such as the Biological Sciences Curriculum Study Course (BSCS), the Chemical Education Materials Study Course (CHEM Study), the Physical Science Study Committee (PSSC), the Chemical Bond Approach (CBA) and the Greater Cleveland Math Program (GCMP).

Book selection committees from the various districts often meet at the IMC to study and make decisions. Teachers also attend the IMC to witness demonstrations of overhead and slide projection, automatic and standard motion picture projectors, and a variety of teaching machines. Later, they are taught to operate this equipment. Study carrels are available for those teachers wishing to explore independent study techniques. Each is equipped with one or more learning devices, such as teaching machines, programmed texts, tape recorders, filmstrip viewers, and so on.

Four full-time artist-technicians provide teachers with a variety of visual materials upon request. The IMC has a well-equipped darkroom and graphic arts studio for this purpose. Visual materials re-

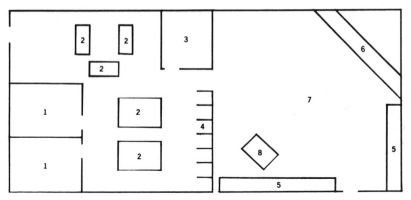

FIGURE ONE
HARKNESS CENTER IMC °
BUFFALO, NEW YORK

1. Offices
2. Filing Cabinets and Storage Cabinets for Equipment
3. Small-Group Discussion Center
4. Electrified Study Carrels
5. District Curriculum Guide Files and Programmed Texts
6. Teaching Wall (built in remote control for projectors and lights)
7. Seats for Large-Group Instruction
8. Remote Control Projectors

° Darkroom, graphic arts, and film library are in separate rooms not shown.

quest forms are kept in each school and may be submitted as frequently as desired. Teachers requiring transparencies, slides, posters, charts or photos merely indicate what they need, describe it on the form, and include a rough sketch to convey their idea. Most orders are filled in less than two weeks after the request has been filed.

The center was organized with the belief that "teachers have neither the time, talent, nor patience to produce their own materials." To back up this claim, the center reports that in one three-month period, several thousand units of educational media were sent to the 105 buildings. However, administrators do agree that if teacher demands become too great for the centralized facility, separate school IMCs should be developed to handle the more immediate teacher requests.

A Centralized IMC in Transition

In Grosse Pointe, Michigan, a once centralized IMC is rapidly moving toward a coordinated system of IMCs. Assisted by three full-time clerks and an A-V technician, the district IMC director maintains close contact with each school IMC. At the elementary level, a resource teacher in each school acts as IMC coordinator. These "elementary resource teachers" are not librarians or A-V technicians, but ex-classroom teachers specially selected for their competence and knowledge in handling both print and nonprint materials. Librarians act as IMC coordinators at the secondary level. All IMC coordinators meet with the district IMC director monthly to set policy and to keep abreast of new developments.

At one time, the IMC book collection contained some 25,000 volumes. In the move toward decentralization, these books were distributed to the various elementary school libraries. Today, all books are processed in the centralized IMC, but none are retained there. Similarly, a collection of 20,000 study prints has been decentralized.

In the film library, which serves all schools, more than 1,200 16mm educational films and 2,200 filmstrips are stored. Almost an equal number of films are rented from various sources during each school year. Daily deliveries are made, upon request, to any of the system's 500 teachers. To speed up processing, film rewind and inspection are accomplished by means of an electronic inspection machine. One clerk is in charge of packing and processing all films. In addition to films and filmstrips, the IMC maintains a collection of models and

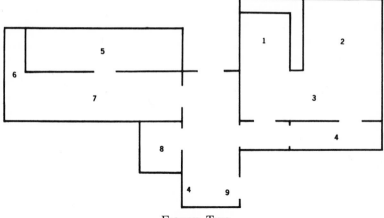

FIGURE TWO
GROSSE POINTE PUBLIC SCHOOLS IMC
GROSSE POINTE, MICHIGAN

1. Office—Coordinator and Secretary
2. Book Processing
3. Transparency Production and Duplicating
4. Storage
5. A-V Technicians' Work Room
6. Film Storage
7. Film Inspection, Repair, and Booking
8. Preview Room
9. Delivery Area

museum pieces which elementary and secondary teachers use for instruction or display.

Each teacher in the district receives an audiovisual catalog which contains lists of all films, filmstrips, models, and museum pieces available in the IMC. Teachers are encouraged to use their catalogs, and all new teachers are given information about the IMC as part of their initial orientation. To exemplify its philosophy, the IMC displays slogans, such as "Set Up for Service to the Classroom Teacher" and "The Right Materials for the Right Child at the Right Time."

An Elementary School IMC

Lomond Elementary School, Shaker Heights, Ohio, provides an excellent example of how a school IMC can improve education in the primary and intermediate grades. In what was originally a traditional library, book stacks were rearranged to divide the room into several small areas. Stacks thus provide visual screening and permit a variety of activities to take place simultaneously without disturbance. Although a modified Dewey Decimal system is used, all stacks and shelves are clearly labeled to designate book classifications. Five carrels, introduced experimentally, have proven so successful that more are planned. "Listening areas," with built-in jacks and earphones, allow students to listen to tapes and records. A filmstrip library also is maintained and students can use individual filmstrip previewers. These previewers and filmstrips, which may be checked out overnight, are especially popular in the intermediate grades 4–6, though many second and third graders also borrow them. Programmed materials on topics such as "Graphing," "Charts and Tables," "Organizing and Reporting," and "Basic Library Skills" are available and are in frequent use. The "story area," carpeted and equipped with screen and overhead projector, is popular with the lower grades. After hearing interesting, illustrated stories, children are anxious to browse and select from the surrounding stacks of primary readers.

The technicians' room, furnished with equipment and materials for making transparencies for the overhead projector, is an always busy location. The technician is ready and willing to produce transparencies for teachers and students or to help them create their own materials.

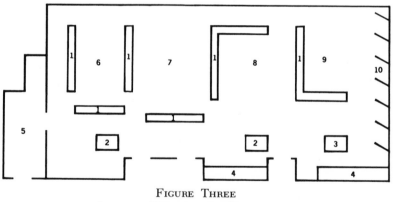

FIGURE THREE
LOMOND ELEMENTARY SCHOOL IMC
SHAKER HEIGHTS, OHIO

1. Stacks
2. Librarians
3. A-V Aide
4. Listening and Viewing Areas
5. Graphic Arts Room
6. Story Area (carpeted)
7. Class and Study Area
8. Independent Study Area
9. Reference Area
10. Study Carrels

With this shift of emphasis from the teaching to the learning process, the former library was renamed the "Learning Center" to better indicate its function. According to the originator of the project: "The real measure of how well we are succeeding, of course, will come in a few years when these children reach high school. I don't doubt that we will be able to tell by the quality of a child's work whether he was in one of these elementary schools with the independent study program. The junior high and high schools are going to be on the spot, and we know it. We are already making changes in their libraries."

A Secondary School IMC

The Hickory Township Senior High IMC, Sharon, Pennsylvania, which began in a small way in 1950, grew in size and scope of service as teachers and pupils saw its value. According to its director, Ronald Green, they are "concerned with the education of the youth through recognition of the needs of the individual and development of attitudes, habits, and understandings essential for a well-adjusted person and a contributing member of our society."

The Senior High IMC operates as a self-sufficient unit serving approximately 1,100 students, and is expected to rely as little as possible upon other centers. The IMC selects and purchases equipment and materials to meet the needs of its own faculty and students. The high school IMC director, who also carries responsibility for "leadership and coordination" of the district program, is assisted by one full-time librarian, one audiovisual coordinator, and one secretary.

The librarian serves as assistant to the director and is responsible for (1) implementing the library program, (2) selecting, training, and supervising student aides, (3) handling public relations, and (4) preparing reports. In addition to her administrative functions, she helps select instructional materials, provides instruction in the use of media, assists in developing standards for the IMC, and participates in curriculum revision and improvements. Much of her time is spent serving pupils and teachers.

The audiovisual coordinator takes prime responsibility for all nonprint materials in the IMC. He also supervises the use of A-V materials and equipment for classroom instruction and helps the staff plan and prepare special audiovisual materials.

The secretary to the director also provides clerical services to the center such as preparation of catalog cards, book pockets, and spine labels.

To supplement the efforts of this limited staff, some 60 student aides volunteer their services throughout the day. They check out materials, repair damaged books, process new materials, prepare bulletin board displays, schedule equipment for use, make classroom deliveries, operate equipment as needed, and prepare simple A-V materials.

The Hickory Township High School IMC contains a number of special purpose rooms. The largest is the main library reading room, which houses some 15,000 volumes. To provide privacy, all but two tables are divided by table top partitions to form study carrels. For informal reading, the room contains three small lounge areas equipped with lounge chairs, end tables, lamps and coffee tables.

All listening and viewing equipment needed for classroom use is stored on open shelves in the audiovisual room. This space, which also serves as a preview area for films, is equipped with two sound proof booths for that purpose. Eighteen listening and viewing stations are located in the individual study room. Two tape decks and one

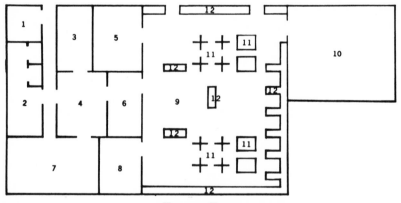

FIGURE FOUR
HICKORY TOWNSHIP HIGH SCHOOL IMC
SHARON, PENNSYLVANIA

1. Darkroom	7. Materials Production
2. Audiovisual Room	8. Curriculum Library
3. Magazine Room	9. Main Library
4. Workroom	10. Library Classroom
5. Individual Study	11. Study Carrels
6. Office	12. Book Shelves

phonograph deck permit a group of students to listen to the same record or tape, or to select from one of three different programs played simultaneously. A special tape recorder, utilizing a one-inch tape, permits a selection from 22 separate 15-minute programs. Teachers find this unit valuable for recording short examinations or special lessons.

The library classroom, adjacent to the main reading room, is used for lectures and film showings. Projectors for 16mm and 35mm are permanently housed in this area and may be operated by remote control from a lectern at the front.

Special curriculum materials and the professional library are housed in a separate room for teachers and library staff. Carpeting, drapes, lounge chairs, and attractive furniture are conducive to browsing or study. The *Education Index* facilitates the use of the many professional journals. Copies of textbooks and the professional vertical file are also located in this room.

The materials production room is used for making posters, charts, transparencies, and slides. A plate maker, duplicator, paper cutter, 35mm camera, dry mount press, air brush, light box, Polaroid copy camera, and a dry-photo copier are available with supplies located in counters under each piece of equipment. Equipment is also provided for making overhead transparencies by means of either diazo or thermographic copiers. For those doing photographic work, a fully equipped darkroom is readily available.

A library workroom is provided for processing and cataloging materials, and a magazine storage room houses five years of back issues. The library is currently receiving 172 magazines, of which 110 are indexed in either the *Reader's Guide to Periodical Literature* or the *Education Index*. In an adjacent room, the 18 most used periodicals and newspapers are available on microfilm. Complete from 1960 to the present, these may be read on any of the three microreader-printers. If a student wishes, he may receive a print-out of any page he is viewing within seconds at no charge.

In the 1967–68 school year the total IMC expenditure per pupil was $8.21, expended as follows:

A-V local materials	$2.51
A-V equipment and repairs	.98
Total A-V	$3.49

Library print materials, local	2.12
Library print materials, ESEA	1.70
Library supplies	.90
Total Library	$4.72
Total IMC	$8.21

In looking to the future, Ronald Green, the director, points out that all Hickory Township High School IMC facilities and services are considered temporary and need to be constantly reevaluated in the light of changing needs. However, he states: "Our experience seems to indicate that teachers who are well oriented to the utilization of the present basic facilities and services will be far better prepared to accept and creatively use some of the more sophisticated devices and media that are currently making their debut."

A Coordinated IMC

In a 1963 doctoral dissertation at the University of Nebraska, Sedley D. Hall made "A Comparative Study of Two Types of Organization of Instructional Materials Centers." His study probed preferences of elementary school teachers toward a centralized plan. He, as a number of other researchers, found that teachers generally consider easy access to materials of primary importance. Reflecting this attitude, recent surveys indicate a trend toward coordinated patterns of operation.

In Rockville, Maryland, the Montgomery County Public Schools have developed a network of IMCs which operate under the aegis of the school system IMC. Prior to July 1961, Montgomery County operated a rather conventional program. A library supervisor and an audiovisual supervisor were assigned to the Department of Educational Services, but operated independently. This system became increasingly ineffective as pupil population and staff needs began to burgeon. At the request of the Superintendent of Schools, the Department of Educational Services, assisted by a professional consultant, undertook a study to determine a more efficient plan of operation. This study led to the development of the present complex of coordinated instructional media centers. The organization is based upon a single salient concept—service. Its motto is "Instructional Materials: The right ones for the right place at the right time."

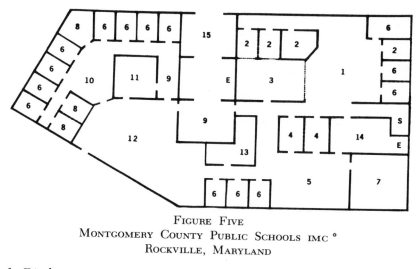

FIGURE FIVE
MONTGOMERY COUNTY PUBLIC SCHOOLS IMC °
ROCKVILLE, MARYLAND

1. Display Area
2. In-Service Education Rooms
3. Rear Projection Room
4. Preview Rooms
5. Reference and Review
6. Offices
7. Mechanical Equipment
8. Conference Rooms
9. Reception Areas
10. Secretaries
11. Duplicating Facilities

12. Curriculum Laboratory
13. Periodical Storage and Work-room
14. Shipping and Receiving
    E—Elevators
    S—Stairway
15. Lobby

° Tape duplicating, graphic arts, and TV studio are in other areas not shown.

To provide such service, each building is encouraged to operate its own IMC. However, a county IMC functions to provide leadership, guidance, and support to the building centers. This County Department of Instructional Materials is responsible for:

1. assisting teachers in use of instructional materials and equipment in the instructional program;

2. coordinating all library, auditory, visual, and related instructional materials and equipment services;

3. developing, in cooperation with the Department of Supervision and Curriculum Development, systematic procedures for the review, evaluation, and selection of instructional materials;

4. coordinating and administering the review, evaluation, and selection of textbooks, instructional materials, and instructional equipment;

5. maintaining a telephone booking service and supplying instructional materials daily to all schools;

6. maintaining a central processing center for all library books and other instructional materials;

7. maintaining a library for the professional staff of the Montgomery County Public Schools;

8. assisting in the development of basic library collections and other collections of instructional materials;

9. assisting all departments in the development of standards and specifications for instructional materials and equipment;

10. assisting the Department of School Facilities in planning new construction.

11. reviewing instructional materials and equipment requisitions and purchase orders in cooperation with the Division of Procurement;

12. coordinating all National Defense Education Act Title III projects in mathematics, science, foreign language, English, reading, history, civics, economics, and geography; Title II, Elementary and Secondary Education Act of 1965; and Section 12, Arts and Humanities Foundation Act;

13. producing selected instructional materials and providing graphic production—design, layout, photography, and typography;

14. providing editing and reproduction services for all printed materials;

15. coordinating all local television production services.

The Department of Instructional Materials is convinced that no school IMC, working alone, could support the extensive program demanded by today's instructional needs.

As a special service that saves time for each school, they point with pride to their central processing system for library books. Orders from individual schools are consolidated and sent to publishers. Upon receipt of books from the suppliers, catalog cards are produced, classification numbers are lettered on the spines, pockets are pasted in, and school ownership is then stamped on each book. The school IMC has only to unpack the books and file the cards.

To speed up the process of distributing items maintained in the central inventory, daily interschool truck delivery service is maintained. Colorcoded catalog cards (showing all materials available in the county IMC) are interfiled in each building IMC card catalog.

Teachers are encouraged to give special requests to the IMC representative in their building, who then telephones the county IMC for immediate confirmation.

Another service is the provision of workshops for teachers, librarians, and administrators. One such workshop was held in response to requests for "an opportunity to learn more about materials and how they can be used in instruction." In the work areas and darkrooms, under the direction of skilled staff members, teachers learned to prepare their own illustrations, transparencies, and films.

As the director facetiously states, ". . . the school library ain't what it used to be." He adds: "I am particularly pleased to report that this is becoming more apparent in our own school system in Montgomery County, Maryland, as we open new buildings with libraries built to allow the underlying principles of an instructional materials center to be fulfilled."

The IMC Concept

The American Association of School Administrators has stated: "Without appropriate materials, a modern educational program is an impossibility. Upon the superintendent falls the task of getting better materials and making them available to teachers." An increasing number of superintendents are accepting this challenge. They see the advantages an IMC offers for the improvement of instruction. They are making the IMC a focal point for individualized instruction—a center where teachers and students can locate every type of information needed for research and study. They are insisting that teachers, librarians, and audiovisual experts work together for the benefit of boys and girls.

We have come a long way from the concept of a library designed as a repository for books to the concept of an IMC designed for students and teachers. However, we must be cognizant of the fact that neither books nor modern media contribute anything to education unless they are properly used. To make the IMC a true "learning center," we must help pupils grow in self-correction, self-analysis, and self-direction. Formal education must culminate, not in a finished body of information, but in the mastery of a method for coping with a lifetime of progress and change.

CHAPTER 6

The Range of Media

by

ROBERT EDWARD FITE

Robert Fite is director of membership for the Department of Audiovisual Instruction of the National Education Association. He has served in various other capacities involving instructional media: assistant in audiovisual laboratories in New York University and Indiana University; chairman of instructional media in a New York school district; and instructor in in-service programs for teachers and librarians.

Dr. Fite holds Ed.S. and Ed.D. degrees from the School of Education, Indiana University. He has been president of the Long Island Educational Communications Council and contributes to professional educational journals.

INSTRUCTIONAL MEDIA CENTERS or learning resource centers should afford the student as well as the teacher an opportunity to learn from the newer materials of instruction. Although the bulk of the world's knowledge is on the printed page, an IMC is more than a library or an audiovisual communications center. The IMC is a place where all the materials of instruction are readily accessible to the learner and a place where students use information and ideas as they see fit. The chains which held the books to the desks in the monastery during the Middle Ages are no longer apropos in meeting the learning needs of those who will be our nation's leaders in the twenty-first century.

It is the purpose of this chapter to give the reader an opportunity to review some of the hardware and software resources which are available as a result of new technological developments. In one sense of the word, the next few pages will be a quick microview of equipment, materials, and educational procedures which, when placed in proper perspective, will serve as a catalyst in the total learning process. These comments are based upon the current writings contained in publications of national education associations, such as the American Library Association, the Association for Supervision and Curriculum Development, the American Association of School Librarians,

The IMC director must be able to communicate easily with students.

and the Department of Audiovisual Instruction of the National Education Association.

It is assumed that the professional staff working in the instructional media center will have a wide knowledge of curriculum, an intimate relationship with learning theory, and a sincere desire to aid both teachers and learners with information regarding the use of media in the solution of instructional problems. It is also assumed that the professional staff will have experience in the routine media service procedures commonly in operation in most libraries and audiovisual centers. Much of the success of the IMC will rest upon the fulcrum of human relations which will be developed by the center director. If the center director does not have a personal interest in working with people and is unable to communicate easily with members of the teaching staff and students, the use of these media will likely be limited. Nothing will ever replace a creative, conscientious, and dedicated teacher. There is no conflict between teachers and machines, but rather there is the opportunity for teachers to become more effective through the use of the power tools of instruction. The media can only enrich, supplement, and make more vivid the subject under discussion. The center director is, in a sense, the broker working with the teacher, information or ideas, and the learner. But a well-meaning director and a sympathetic teacher are not enough to insure a good IMC. Adequate physical facilities, adequate budget, adequate professional staff, and an adequate line of authority are all essential to implement desired educational services if the center is to meet the challenges placed before it.

Media Center Staffing

The American Association of School Librarians and the Department of Audiovisual Instruction of the National Education Association recently published the new *National Standards for School Media Programs*. Technological change is occurring so rapidly that these standards will be reviewed every two years. These new standards attempt to define the terms, describe the professional tasks, and indicate the scope of both print and nonprint media.

The Department of Audiovisual Instruction of the NEA position paper, entitled *The Role of the Media Specialist,* carefully delineates the various tasks for a media professional to perform on a building, district, county, or regional level, a state or federal level, and a college or university level position. The paid professional role of the media specialist demands an intimate knowledge of curriculum, the learning process, behavioristic psychology, and the resulting change process. Within his professional preparation must be a knowledge of the media and their application in the learning process.

Media staff members must be capable of understanding the needs of administrators, teachers, and students, competent in relating research findings to media utilization, and competent in managing and organizing the instructional media center. Media staff members must have a knowledge of budgetary management and insure that the technological equipment used in the instructional media center is maintained at a high level of operation efficiency. Media staff members must take the necessary action to provide information to teachers and students concerning new teaching media and to keep the administration informed as to new technological developments which could have a direct influence upon the total instructional program of the school.

No one knows for certain what will be required of the media specialist in the future. The physical plant, the hardware, and an adequate budget may be available, but the essential ingredient in making the instructional media center relevant will probably rest with the professional staff.

Study Carrels

Provision should be made in the instructional media center for individual study carrels as well as for large areas of study. A study carrel is a piece of furniture which affords the student a degree of privacy to work and learn independently or with one or more fellow students. Study carrels may be simple table-like structures with three enclosed sides or they may be highly sophisticated items of furniture which permit the use of electronic devices. A study carrel may be so designed that it serves as a "home base" for students who desire to use portable tape recorders, record players, teaching machines, typewriters, microfilm readers, small movie projectors, filmstrip projectors, slide viewers, and even portable television sets. These carrels are designed with a high degree of electronic sophistication and have learning systems built into them. Some carrels provide two-way communications systems with the resource media specialist who is assigned to the instructional media center.

The environment of the instructional media center is conducive to the assimilation of information. Modern educational media can challenge the student by insuring an opportunity for the more rapid retrieval of information than is commonly provided through conventional means. It has been shown that a film can bring more understanding to students than some books can. Machine programmed learning can give more logical understanding of a concept than

A student uses a film in an individual study carrel.

some detailed explanations can provide. A rerun of a videotape can provide some straight-lined explanations that were not achieved in the first viewing. A fully equipped electronic study carrel makes these learning opportunities and many more available to the concerned student.

All too often the media specialist has been asked to police the students in the library reading room instead of giving assistance in finding new and improved materials of instruction. A typical situation generally involves a few students busily engaged in reading while the majority of students are looking at each other and talking. Study carrels cannot guarantee that a student will refrain from daydreaming, but they do give the learner an increased opportunity to improve his study skills.

Programmed Instruction

In this age when educational psychologists are discussing the value of discovery type learning, instructional media specialists must recognize that a bridge has been built between the psychological laboratory and the classroom. No longer must either of these areas exist in isolation, but rather, with the research proving the effectiveness of programmed instruction, the individual student is afforded a new pathway toward improved learning. Programmed instruction permits the student to move ahead at his own pace of learning, to have immediate reinforcement of learning, and to study without the direct control of a classroom teacher.

The instructional media center can readily offer the functional means of bringing together the concerned student with the teaching machine or other modes of programmed learning. There are a number of quality publishers and authors who have adequately researched their programs of learning for all levels of instruction. It would be outside the realm of this chapter to discuss grade-level utilization or subject-matter content for programmed instruction. The reader is referred to publications on the subject distributed by the American Institute for Research, the Fund for Advancement of Education, the American Educational Research Association, and the National Society for Programmed Instruction.

Computer-assisted instruction is now part of the educational spectrum. CAI is several levels above current programmed learning.

Many of the programmed learning courses have been converted to the language of the computer and now afford the student a greater sophistication in meeting individual ways of learning. In a few years, CAI will be able to react rapidly with the experience of the learner. Relevant data, such as the student's I.Q., socioeconomic setting, vocabulary level, motivation, and so on, will play a part in selecting the sequences that best fit the student's individual learning process.

Computer-assisted instruction may very well bring about startling changes in the IMC environment. Within the next few years, the media center consultant's role may dramatically change to that of a programmer and a diagnostician of individual learning problems. At this time in our historical development of instructional technology, it is impossible to say when this new type of activity will take form and to what depth and scope this new learning technique will evolve. We are able to state that more intellectually appealing programs are being developed and that the technology is rapidly permitting the fullest exploitation of the most creative ideas.

Language Laboratories

A majority of the universities, colleges, and secondary schools in the United States have an instructional area known as the language laboratory. It provides facilities for the use of tapes and recordings in a teaching-learning situation. In the language laboratory, too often the learner is participating under close instructor surveillance and is seldom given the privilege of reviewing and enriching his knowledge of the language during unscheduled periods. It is unfortunate when thousands of dollars have been expended by school purchasing agents to procure reels of prerecorded tapes which are stored in locked cabinets for the major portion of the academic year.

Four years of research, 1959–63, by the Bureau of Audiovisual Instruction, Board of Education of the City of New York for the New York State Education Department, documents the thesis that language laboratories do aid in the learning and retention of a foreign language. Comparison between the student who studied with the assistance of a language laboratory and the conventionally taught student, shows that a greater percentage of the former continued their study of language into the optional fourth year.

A few years ago, one language teacher asked, "Why stop with just language laboratories?" The point was that a good language laboratory should combine the features and functions of a library, a study hall, and a regular classroom. This creation of an electronic study center demands a complexity of uses. Students of English, literature, poetry, history, government, economics, business education, science, speech, and music would be involved in directed learning experiences in this electronic study center. The innovative instructor's role would be one of programming short segments of his course and providing his students with a question and response tape.

The electronic laboratory is not limited in its service to any single curriculum. Nor has the electronic laboratory hamstrung the faculty; rather, it has permitted the instructor to become more flexible and more creative. Since the instructional media specialist is not necessarily a subject-matter expert, it would be mere folly to suggest that he make decisions regarding a particular design or singular function of the electronic laboratory units. The decision as to the design of the unit and its capability must originate from responsible faculty members.

Good instruction requires money, and educators should not apolo

Directed learning experiences in an electronic study center.

gize for expenditures to maintain the purchased instructional equipment. It is the professional responsibility of the media specialist to insure that good operational care be given to the equipment and materials and that the necessary controls be established for the prevention of malicious handling. An electronic laboratory is the same as any mechanical tool and should be modified, improved, and, if necessary, replaced when a better one is available. Very few of us are eager to drive a car which is over ten years old. Why then should we settle for electronic equipment which has become obsolete and is not capable of meeting the educational potentials available through more current and improved teaching tools?

Educational Television and Telelecture

Educational institutions in every part of the United States have overwhelmingly affirmed that students can learn effectively from television. It is concluded from one comprehensive analysis of many research studies that over 20 percent of the observed students learned significantly more from the use of television than from conventional classroom teaching. Class size generally had little to do with learning via television, and students and teachers generally reacted more favorably toward television in the lower grades than those in high school and college classes. Television has been able to multiply and magnify curriculum content.

Low-cost videotape recorders make television accessible to every learning situation for the viewing of both network and locally produced programs. Many state education departments permit educators to duplicate portions of their videotape library. Prerecorded videotape is now available from various sources for use in the instructional program.

Educational television is part of an instructional system whose basic effectiveness has been proven. Like any other instructional tool, application and growth of the medium depend upon the one who designs the message and the learner who comes in contact with the message. The full potential of educational television has not yet been achieved because of the continuing development of educational technology and the need for more knowledge about the total learning process.

In like manner, the telelecture, which is available wherever there are telephones, should be coordinated by the instructional media specialist. The telelecture is a unique concept in educational communications, which is made feasible through low cost. This communications technique brings to the class the voices of resource personnel who are not available in the immediate area. These telelectures can add new dimensions to the instructional program because of the ease of arrangement. Within a few years, educational technology may have moved to the point where the live visual will accompany the audio message via telephone lines at cost compatible with current charges.

Microfilm

Storage space is generally at a premium in the average instructional media center. Gutenberg and his internationally famous fifteenth-century invention—the printing press—gave to the 3,000-year-old medium—paper—the responsibility for storing man's knowledge. With the advent of computer technology and the storage capabilities of microfilm, the role of paper is being reevaluated by all elements of our society.

It has been said that all the millions of books currently stored on the approximately 300 miles of shelving in the Library of Congress could be reproduced on acetate and stored in six standard filing cabinets. In a recent visit to the Library of Congress, the writer found that the average time for obtaining a book from the stacks was forty-five minutes.

In this A-bomb, push-button century, there is no justification for inefficiency with information retrieval. It is extremely difficult to justify expenditures for large sums of money for space allocation, personnel, and furniture if stored information cannot be made easily available to the learner.

Few school systems make back issues of the *New York Times* and other well-known journals available. The high school student is generally advised by the school librarian to visit the public library to obtain news articles. The IMC should have the means and capability to meet the needs of the learner instead of transmitting these responsibilities by default to the public library. This is easily accomplished by means of microfilm. For example, a complete year of *National Geographic* is contained in one small microfilm. All that is required is a microfilm reader to enlarge the image. Such readers are available

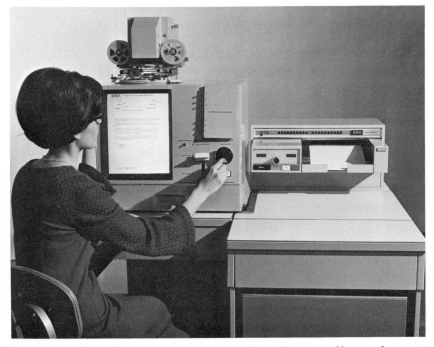

Printed copies can be easily obtained from the microfilm reader.

for as little as $100. Microfilm readers permit the student to read via magnification of the data on the acetate and, if he desires, to secure a printed copy of the data by just pushing one or two buttons. This copy is made on a paper which has an emulsion base and thus may be utilized by the learner for a number of years.

Recently a breakthrough has been noted in the information storage system which permits up to 3,200 8½ × 11-inch pages of copy, line, and halftone art to be stored on a 4 × 6-inch transparency. This transparency, which has an indefinite life, may be laminated on both front and back. The lamination will protect the message from scratches, dirt, and grease. Hard copies of any page may be reproduced. This 4 × 6-inch transparency has been referred to as microfiche or microform.

What are the future possibilities of this type of information storage system? Ideas for both schools and industry come readily to mind:

1. Complete medical histories of an individual or a family could be stored on microfiche and maintained in a central clearing house.

2. Detailed lesson plans for an entire grade level or academic disci-

pline could be placed on microfiche and stored for future reference.

3. In the military or in business and industry, where long and detailed written operational procedures are necessary to the successful functioning of the organization, storage via microfiche affords greater dissemination of the written procedure. Each subsection could have its own microfiche and have the availability of a low-cost microfiche reader within a few steps of the operating section.

4. In the field of vocational education, lengthy training manuals and parts catalogs could have their contents stored on microfiche and be readily accessible to the instructor and student.

5. The entire works of Dickens, Shakespeare, and Hemingway would fill but a single transparency.

This kind of stored data coupled with the capability of an IBM card affords the learner a rapid retrieval of written and statistical information. Obviously, the uses of microfiche are endless and have just begun to be tapped.

Facilities for Student Viewing
of Films and Filmstrips

In a manner similar to that of the portable language laboratory, educators should consider the feasibility of making available to the students filmstrips, slides, and films. The educational film producer has spent thousands of dollars in order to guarantee a quality product for the distribution of classroom information. It is not uncommon for some educational films to require a budget of $50,000 to $100,000 before one single cent of revenue has been returned to the producer. Under proper control and supervision, the educational film and filmstrip can and should be used by the interested student on an individual basis.

There are a number of rear projection machines and devices which permit daylight viewing of projected visuals. The instructional media center could easily be provided with a jackbox and several headsets in order to permit students to view 8mm or 16mm sound films without disturbing others in the area.

Various schools are utilizing 8mm single-concept films for independent study with individual students. These films are projected from a cartridge which may run as long as thirty minutes. The average 8mm loop-film runs from two to four minutes and generally permits the stu-

A film can and should be used by the interested student.

dent to still frame the image for a more detailed examination of the projection. These films may be projected via a rear screen which allows daylight viewing. A projector for 8mm loop-film costs less than $75.

The 8mm educational film has become an important part of the IMC. Educators may locally produce their own 8mm sound films without special knowledge of photographic techniques and sound reproduction. Both Kodak and Fairchild have an 8mm camera and recorder on the market which sells for less than $700.

A student may use educational filmstrips either in the instructional media center or in his home. Circulating filmstrips and viewers outside the IMC enables the students to study and review the filmstrips at home in a manner similar to that of print materials. If sound filmstrips are circulated to the students, a record player should be provided for home usage.

Local Production Facilities

The instructional media center should be a place where teachers and students alike may produce teaching and learning materials. One of the most useful but simple devices is the thermographic copier. In a matter of seconds, newspaper or magazine pictures may be copied or turned into visuals for projection. Although such a machine enables teachers to produce overhead transparencies quickly and inexpensively, there are still too many school administrators who foolishly consider any type of reproduction, whether it is the overhead transparency, mimeograph, or ditto, too costly to use freely.

Lettering facilities for bulletin board displays, posters, and flashcards are an integral part of the production facilities. LeRoy, Wrico, and similar lettering devices may be used to create attractive signs. The finished product may then be used in making overhead transparencies, dry or wet mount displays, or lettering for titles in the production of sound/slide or motion picture films.

Dry mounting and wet mounting are not difficult processes for most teachers to produce. In the wet mount process, one places rubber cement on a board, applies a sheet of waxed paper over the coated area, and then centers the item to be adhered in the proper position. Once this is done, the waxed paper is removed by sliding it out from under the item to be mounted. In dry mounting, one places a piece of dry mount tissue between the material to be mounted and the material upon which it is to be mounted. Heat is then applied with a hot press or hot iron. With a hot press one can laminate a thin sheet of plastic over wood, metal, or paper in order to prevent damage to the surface of the article. These processes and others for locally producing instructional media are graphically described by Minor and Frye in their recent book on production techniques.[1]

The staff of the instructional media center should recognize that not all teacher-made materials are created within the school. Some valuable learning areas exist in various places throughout the community. It is not always feasible or possible to take the learner to these areas; therefore, they must be brought to the learner.

The forward-thinking instructional media specialist will make available to the teaching staff 8mm, 16mm and 35mm cameras plus film and support services for the processing and developing of the finished product. In most cases, the exposed film may be shipped out to a local film laboratory for a small expenditure. A few years ago, Dr. Land developed the Polaroid camera; today many types of polaroid film, both color and black and white, are available. Polaroid prints may be used for bulletin board displays, supporting visuals for press releases, and direct teaching materials. Polaroid also has the capability of placing negatives on an overhead master along with lettering paste-ups. The finished product lends a professional appearance to overhead transparencies.

Facilities for tape preparation, dubbing of the voice, music, and sound effects to the master tape are necessary services to be provided by the instructional media center's staff. These machines and devices are not highly complex, but they offer to every teacher and student an opportunity to produce locally an audio device for classroom enrichment.

In-Service Education

The instructional media specialist must make the school board and the chief school administrator aware of the value of in-service education. It is imperative that administrators, curriculum specialists, and classroom teachers be given an opportunity to work with all types of instructional materials and media. If positive results are to be achieved from the in-service education program, those in attendance must learn more than how to operate the equipment and produce the instructional materials. They must also be given exposure to the area of behavioral objectives and message design.

Research has shown that four years of college-level academic preparation does not necessarily insure that a teacher has knowledge of the application and utilization of modern educational technology. A teacher who wholly relies upon the mere verbal presentation of a topic and, because of inadequate training or indifference to the use of instructional media, does not use the resources afforded him through the instructional media center, is not giving the learner the advantage of the multiplicity of available instructional resources.

Professional IMC staff members must be allocated time to meet faculty members on a person-to-person basis in order to discuss curricular needs. The administrative structure of any educational institution must be cognizant of task distribution and time allocation. If an in-service education program is to achieve academically respectable results, then time must be provided for the IMC specialist to share information regarding the selection and evaluation of both print and nonprint materials. Time must be made available to the IMC specialist for the purpose of keeping specific learning goals in proper focus and of recycling additional services when the teaching-learning process demands it. In-service education does not necessarily have to be limited to a formal 15-week college course but may be tailored to make provision for short clinics or briefings to the concerned persons.

Students who are not receiving instruction as a result of the new media and materials of learning will be seriously handicapped when they leave the classroom to assume their responsibilities in society. We are on the threshold of bringing a more meaningful learning program to the students than at any other time in our history. The problems and discouragements which the instructional media specialist faces are many, but our youth deserve the privilege of learning from any technological device which will assist in winning the battle against poverty, ignorance, and hatred.

CHAPTER 7

The Range of Services

by

LeRoy R. Lindeman

*As the administrator of the Divisions of Instructional Media
for the Utah State Board of Education, LeRoy R. Lindeman
is responsible for audiovisual and library instruction, programmed learning, and educational television in the schools
of Utah.*

*Dr. Lindeman, who holds a doctorate in educational ad-
ministration with emphasis on media, has taught on the elementary and secondary levels and was the director of educational media services at Brigham Young University. He has
contributed articles to several periodicals, including the*
Utah Educational Review *and* Educational Screen and A-V
Guide.

For CENTURIES man has attempted to teach his progeny utilizing
whatever techniques and devices were at his command. Originally
the teaching was in the open, and all of nature was available for illustrations and examples. As civilization progressed, he developed
special places for learning. Before long the teacher found himself rele-
gated to a teaching station composed of four walls and sometimes little
more. A hundred years ago this was adequate, as education was limited to the few and the curriculum was a very narrow treatment of
selected basic subjects, many of which had little direct relationship to
the everyday world. The written word alone provided the needed
information for the scholar.

During the past 60 years we have witnessed virtually a knowledge

LAWYER	SCIENTIST	DOCTOR
2,200,000 New Opinions	60,000 to 100,000 Articles	3/4 New Prescriptions non-existent 25 years ago

Problems of Keeping Up

explosion. Publications, which had been doubling in number every 45 years, now are doubling every five years.[1] Radios and television sets, nonexistent at the turn of the century, are in over 50,000,000 homes in the United States.[2] Two million two-hundred thousand court decisions affecting our lives are handed down every year. From 60,000 to 100,000 scientific articles are published annually, and three out of every four prescriptions now being filled were not available 25 years ago.[3] Fifty percent of the positions college graduates are now filling were not in existence when these students were born.[4] The problem of transmitting this knowledge has become no mean task.

These new challenges have presented and are creating a new outlook in education. Horse and buggy teaching methods are as obsolete as horse and buggy methods of transportation. Teachers have adopted new techniques which have proven to be more effective and efficient. Those new techniques have required the use of many technological aids—some created just for this purpose within the past decade. The teacher of today is rapidly becoming "a professional" highly skilled in the techniques of communication.

Administrators generally have recognized the changes in teaching techniques and have taken steps to provide the teacher with the necessary technological materials and equipment. One relatively new development emerging in education today is that of the instructional media or materials center. It embodies within it the concept of a total resource center wherein all instructional media, equipment, and services are available to both the teacher and the student. It is a place where facilities are so arranged that not only the books and printed matter of the typical library are available, but also the newer media such as motion pictures, filmstrips, tape and disc recordings, and facilities and equipment for teachers and students to create their own teaching tools. While a relatively new idea, it is catching on and many areas are adopting the practice with an enthusiasm not often found in educational ranks. In a recent national study by Lindeman,[5] 78 percent of the experts responding indicated that separate library and other learning resource centers should be integrated into an instructional media center and located within each school.

Types of Services

CIRCULATION

One of the major services usually provided by an instructional media center is the circulation of instructional media and equipment. The checking in and out of printed matter such as books and pamphlets to individual students and teachers for a specified period of time, usually associated with most libraries, is a part of the services now being rendered by most instructional media centers. Printed materials of this type are usually provided on a short-term basis of from one to three hours as well as for extended usage up to two weeks in length. This service is provided for individuals for their personal use. Many instructional media centers also circulate collections of books on a particular subject or grade level to individual classrooms to provide immediate reference material for any particular unit of study. Davis County School District, located in Utah just north of Salt Lake City, prepares collections of up to 30 different books for any teacher in the district. The teacher may then keep this collection in his classroom as long as he likes up to the end of the school year, or he may exchange it for another set as often as every 30 days. The teacher is even permitted to search the stacks himself and personally select the individual titles for the collection.

Individual pictures and sets of pictures are often included in the collections of instructional media centers. These pictures are usually

Picture Sets

mounted to protect them from wear and to extend their useful life. Many centers have found the lamination—mounting in plastic—of pictures to be the most satisfactory way of preserving them when both the long-range cost and the heavy use are considered. These are usually circulated on the same basis as books and pamphlets.

Recordings of various types are beginning to play an increasingly important role in education and are taking their place in the center. The new technological developments now make it possible for individuals or groups to hear world-famous symphony orchestras or recent Broadway plays in full stereophonic high-fidelity sound. Many centers now make both record and tape recordings available to students and teachers for extended loan periods. Some centers provide a tape duplication service and, where no copyrights are involved, they copy programs on a separate tape or cassette for individual use. New developments in the electronics field now permit mass duplication of up to 10 copies of any taped program in a matter of minutes. The student of tomorrow may find a small portable tape recorder as vital to him as his pencil.

Another basic component of an instructional media center is a filmstrip and/or slide-set collection. These photographic materials provide numerous colored illustrations invaluable in clarifying and explaining

Student Using Filmstrip

many of the teaching concepts basic in today's educational program. While some schools permit selected filmstrips to be stored in the individual classroom, most items of this type are maintained and circulated by the instructional media center. In the past they have been restricted to group usage, but recent trends indicate a much heavier usage by individuals. The centers are meeting this demand by providing filmstrip viewers and projectors for the use of both teachers and students.

Large centers also maintain basic collections of motion pictures. However, these require special care in both storing and handling and, unless the center is quite large, it is usually wiser to obtain motion picture films from district, regional, or university centers which can afford the necessary equipment to properly circulate films and have the necessary volume to justify such an expenditure. Attempting to maintain collections of motion picture films without proper care is unwise from both an economical and utilization standpoint. Films wear out rapidly, and teachers become discouraged when they receive films which do not project properly or films whose continuity disrupts rather than contributes to learning. Most instructional media centers within schools act as a clearing house which orders, obtains, and returns films for teachers. Until now, this service usually has been limited to teachers; however, recent developments are now broadening the horizon, and soon it may be economically feasible to provide this service for individual student use.

Recently another medium, not previously included in the instructional materials field, has emerged and is rapidly finding a place in education. The 8mm film, long used for home movies, has matured, and recent engineering progress has made possible a lightweight, inexpensive, cartridge-loaded projector. The combination has created a tremendous interest in the use of a short film covering only one phase or step—the single-concept film. Nearly all film producers are now heavily committed to the production of films of this type, and many schools are purchasing them for the use of both teachers and students.

Some centers also circulate teaching kits of various types. The Los Angeles City System produces many kits for just this purpose. Teaching kits contain a variety of instructional media including flat pictures, filmstrips, recordings, and realia items, such as articles of clothing, coins, handicraft samples, and so on.

The circulation of motion picture films, filmstrips, and recordings poses a new problem for the instructional media administrator. Unlike books, these items are usually scheduled for a much shorter period of time and it is more critical that they be utilized at just the

Single-Concept Loop Film

right moment. This means that some provision for advance scheduling must be made. Some teachers wish to schedule items as much as several months in advance of the actual use date. These media must also be inspected closely for damage and repaired after every usage if they are to be effectively and economically utilized. New technological developments now permit this to be accomplished rapidly through the use of electronic equipment. Time for this inspection and repair must be calculated in the schedule. Customers scheduling in advance need written confirmation of their order to assist them in remembering and planning.

The instructional media center also circulates projectors, record players, and tape recorders. These become necessities when one recognizes that a motion picture film in and of itself is of little value. In order to view it, one must have a projector of the right type, size, and style. In addition to the equipment needed for utilizing instructional media, many pieces of equipment which by themselves can improve the teaching situation are usually provided by instructional media centers. The overhead projector, the opaque projector, and the tape recorder are often used with teacher-made media. While many schools are now equipping each classroom with an overhead projector and other selected equipment, the role of the center is to provide supplemental equipment as well as the basic needs of classrooms and areas not so equipped.

A comparatively recent innovation in the circulation of instructional materials is the use of closed-circuit television. A number of schools have been wired with cables which permit the pick-up of programs in the instructional media center as well as in selected remote areas and the feeding of this signal to television sets in selected classrooms. This system not only permits the viewing of live programs from several locations, but also permits the distribution of motion pictures, filmstrips, slides, and recordings via the cable rather than physical transportation.

REFERENCE

Another type of service usually provided in an instructional media center is the provision for individual study. The reference materials usually associated with a library—books, periodicals, encyclopedias, indexes, and so on—are all included. In addition, facilities must be provided for viewing projected materials and listening to audio recordings.

Quiet Listening with Tape Recorder and Earphones

Many centers provide an area equipped with tape recorders and record players to which earphones have been attached. A number of pieces of equipment are available which permit several students to listen quietly to the same selection. Other centers provide listening facilities in rather unique ways. For example, at Brigham Young University the entire listening operation has been engineered and installed so that the student never actually handles the recording. The media are all cataloged in the master catalog as well as in a special listening-card catalog. The student or teacher selects the title and call number of the desired recording and gives information to the librarian. The student is given a headset and instructed to plug it into a specific channel. Each listening station is equipped for handling 18 different stereophonic channels, with separate volume controls for each ear. While the student is locating a vacant station, the media coordinator obtains the desired recording and places it on the master for the channel designated. Some channels are equipped with tape recorders and others with record turntables. Currently, 18 program channels and 84 student stations are in operation.

Many of the programs used are commercially prepared. However, the flexibility of magnetic recording makes possible the use of many teacher-made recordings. The teacher often includes excerpts illustrating specific points. The expansion of the classroom to an almost

Scheduling Program and Receiving Earphones at Brigham Young University's Listening Library

personalized tutoring session has been well accepted by the teachers and students at Brigham Young University. After only a few years of operation, the facilities were overtaxed and plans were developed to double the number of channels and the number of listening stations.

Recently, Brigham Young University installed an audio and video cable system linking all buildings on campus together in a spider-web of wires. From a central distribution center, audio and video programs can be fed to almost any location on campus. Every major assembly room and classroom is a potential listening or viewing station. Stereophonic programs originating in the listening area can also be fed into this system, and additional listening stations are being located all over the campus. Some of these stations will be located within the dormitories. Investigation shows that it is even feasible to

connect the audio portion of this system into the commercial telephone system. This makes every telephone on the local exchange a
listening station. A few years ago an experimental program providing
a 10-minute recording in a foreign language met with considerable
success. The teacher recorded specific information on tape. Included
in this recording was specific information on which the teacher later
quizzed the students. By dialing a particular number, each student
could hear the recording. It was available to him from any telephone
in the area and at any time of the day or night. If he wanted to review or repeat it, all he had to do was redial the number. The major
limitations of this program were the quality of the sound and the
fact that it had to be monaural. This eliminated the possibility of
using the system for musical selections.

Facilities must also be provided for viewing filmstrips, slides, and
motion pictures. Small viewers have long been available for individualized study of filmstrips and slides. On the other hand, motion pictures have required special facilities. Centers across the country have
alleviated this viewing problem in several ways. Some have equipped
special rooms for screening the films. In some cases these have been

Individual Student Listening Station at Brigham Young University's Listening Library

Tape and Record Console in Listening Library

small theaters seating up to 25 or 30 persons. Others have obtained projectors with built-in rear projection screens or have purchased separate rear projection units. Because of the cost of these facilities, the use of the media has been somewhat restricted, usually limited to teachers and small groups. This type of individualized service has been limited to printed matter in the past. Now students are able not only to survey the books in the field, but also to view many education films and filmstrips and to utilize the recorded resources. The teacher of today is not limited to the four walls of the classroom and to the written pages between the covers of a book. The entire world of sight and sound can now become the stage of learning.

Production

A third major function of an instructional media center is to provide facilities for the teacher and/or student to make instructional media. In the study conducted by Lindeman [6] the following production facilities were recommended by the group of experts surveyed.

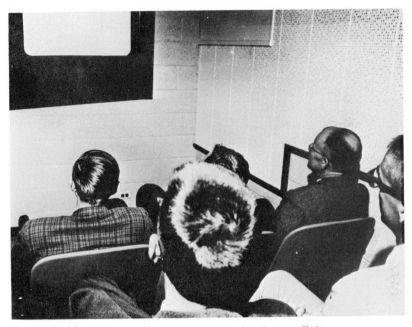

Preview Room for Screening of Films by Small Groups

Rear Projection Unit for Screening Films in Open Areas

1. Basic mounting facilities. The experts generally agree that every school instructional media center should provide facilities and equipment for mounting flat materials such as pictures, maps, and charts. This includes dry mount presses, rubber cement dispensers, mounting boards, muslin, wheat paste, paper cutters, and such other materials and equipment as are necessary.

2. Overhead transparencies. Facilities also should be provided for the preparation and production of overhead transparencies. Cardboard mounts, clear and frosted acetate, samples of clip art, infra-red and/or diazo copying machines, etc. are needed as well as space for preparing the materials.

3. Lettering. A drawing table and various types of lettering devices also are recommended. This includes pen and ink, rubber stamps, stencils, cut-out letters, and such mechanical devices as the Wrico, LeRoy, and Varigraph.

4. Coloring. Facilities and materials for coloring instructional materials are recommended as an integral part of any center. Coloring media for posters and charts and for overhead transparencies are needed. Poster paints, water colors, pastels, colored inks, felt tip pens, colored adhesive acetate sheets, and other similar materials make a wide variety of materials available for the teacher.

Drawing Table

5. Duplicating. Some type of duplicating facility should be provided. This might range from a spirit duplicator to a multilith press. In smaller centers, the spirit duplicator suffices.

The experts indicated that the following facilities should be provided in large centers but probably should not be included in smaller centers:

6. High contrast photography. A darkroom, an enlarger, cameras, photographic papers, and the necessary chemicals are needed to provide this facility. As the use of photographic techniques involves some skill, someone on the center staff should be familiar with and able to supervise all photographic services and facilities in order to prevent waste and discouragement.

7. Copying facilities. The ability to copy pictures, maps, charts, etc. on small slides can be of real value to the educator. However, again some skill is needed, and these facilities should be provided only where trained personnel are available.

KEY TO MATERIALS

Somehow all these materials must be organized so that the student can easily find what he needs. In most centers the card catalog is currently the key which opens the doors to learning. All materials should be listed by subject as well as by title and author when appropriate. Many centers color code their cards for easy identification. Tomorrow the computer may replace the card catalog, bringing information to the student in microseconds in more detail than the best of today's card catalogs.

PERSONNEL

No center can function without adequate personnel. The instructional media center calls for a professional educator at its helm. He should have training in the total media field—library science, audiovisual communication, educational television, curriculum, and administration. Supporting him will be a team of experts, including additional media specialists in large schools, and the necessary technical and clerical personnel to perform the many and varied responsibilities assigned the center. Several states are redoing their certification

The Key to the IMC

requirements to provide for this media generalist. In 1968, Utah adopted such a program, eliminating the separate certificates for librarians and other media personnel. Other states are following this pattern.

Summary and Challenge

With the explosion of knowledge we are now experiencing, the instructional media field is undergoing a rapid change. Related fields are merging their facilities in order to provide better service to their consumers. New specialties are emerging. The instructional media center of today is a far cry from the closet of yesterday which stored A-V equipment occasionally used by some bold teacher. It is reasonable to expect the center of tomorrow will likewise be radically different. The circulation of projected and audio media may become entirely electronic, with the teacher of tomorrow calling upon the resources of an entire collection by merely dialing a predetermined number from his teaching console. The trend is definitely toward expanding the types of collections, particularly in a local or school center.

The combining of typical library and audiovisual services into an instructional media center serving both teachers and pupils will provide a wealth of printed and audiovisual materials for the conscientious educator and student. Provisions for individualized study and instruction will be readily available in tomorrow's centers—although physically they may be located in separate buildings which may even be in a city some distance from the actual media being used. Through the use of electronic data retrieval techniques, printed annotated lists on any particular subject will be available. Much of the laborious task of searching will thus be eliminated and the educator will have at his fingertips the accumulated knowledge of the world ready for his personal analysis and study.

Developments in production techniques will make it possible for the educator to reproduce in full color in a matter of seconds any visual media he desires for use in his classroom. The audio field will continue to grow, making it possible by the flick of a switch or the pushing of a button to fill a classroom with stereophonic high fidelity sound carefully selected to create the right atmosphere and communicate the desired concept to the students.

The educator of tomorrow will be limited only by his imagination. Through the facilities and trained personnel of the instructional media center, the four walls of his classroom will vanish and the world will become his stage for learning. The entire pattern of education will change from the regimented, formalized 50-minute-period group-lecture to free, carefully selected multisensory individualized experiences for each student. The technology of today will be utilized to build a greater tomorrow.

CHAPTER 8

Implementing an IMC

by

HERSCHEL V. ROWE

Herschel V. Rowe, the assistant superintendent of the Leyden High School District in the suburbs of Chicago, is a pioneer in the movement for instructional media centers. He started his teaching career at the age of 19 in a one-room school and later served as a high school chemistry teacher before turning his talent to school administration. He was the first principal of West Leyden High School, Northlake, Illinois, a school recognized for its IMC since 1958.

Dr. Rowe holds an M.S. and an Ed.D. from the University of Illinois. He has used the ideas in his doctoral thesis, which centered around the employment of two-way communication for task-force efficiency, to develop the team approach in implementing an IMC.

ALTHOUGH MOST AIMS of instructional media centers are not new, the implementation of this concept of organized teaching materials has increased at a rapid pace during the past five years. Such methods of instruction as team teaching, programmed learning, independent study, large-group instruction, and closed-circuit television have undoubtedly fostered considerable enthusiasm for the development of IMCs. This trend is definitely directed toward the establishment of an area in the school as a laboratory for learning with appropriate equipment and a competent staff. Many areas of the high school curriculum, such as home economics, industrial arts, physical education, science, and business education have well-developed self-contained laboratories. Other curricular areas such as English, social studies,

108

and mathematics have not. Sometimes the availability of reference books, films, and records is limited, and these basic materials have, in years past, been poorly organized for maximum use.

The emphasis being placed on the instructional media center may well be the most significant movement in education for many years. In its fullest meaning the IMC is a true learning laboratory, a center for all departments of the school, a place with facilities and staff available for planning as well as execution, an environment that will give a fresh perspective on learning. It implies the best in teaching and the extensive use of available written, visual, and auditory materials to make learning vital and realistic. For many years the school library was severely limited in scope, but it can become a laboratory for learning and a center for new developments in learning, if school leaders set the stage for its use.

Undoubtedly, many administrators have not fully visualized the potential of an instructional media center. They may think of it as a minor revision of the school library or perhaps a mere combination of the library and the audiovisual department, both admittedly desirable programs but limited in scope. This chapter will focus on the administrator's role in the development of the instructional media center, explaining how he serves as a catalyst in its promotion and sets the stage for acceptance.

Role of the Administrator

As the administrator and his staff plan the physical setting of the IMC, set the climate for change, involve teachers, employ staff, and sell the whole idea to the board of education, the administrator's personality, attitudes, and techniques of human relations become evident and contribute to the success or failure of the endeavor. This is a prime example of a task force in action and as such requires positive, capable leadership.

The administrator must recognize his role and encourage communication within the administrative hierarchy. The school principal, as an educational leader, is midway between the specialist on his staff and the forces responsible for financial control. The situation becomes even more complex for the superintendent of a large school system. In organizing a centrally located instructional media center to serve many schools, the superintendent knows that expensive physical equipment will be of little value unless there is a cooperative desire to make full use of it.

The success of an administrator is closely related to his ability to set up channels through which ideas flow freely to him from teachers, students, and parents. Communication of this sort is never easy, and an atmosphere of free exchange is indeed rare. We must start with the assumption that maximum involvement is needed, that ideas from those directly involved in the classroom are fundamental.

Even though some suggestions from staff members may appear to be impractical, complete disregard of any idea tends to produce a negative effect on the initiator. In rejecting any suggestion, the administrator must be careful not to give the impression that he would be unreceptive to future suggestions, and he must be prepared to give valid reasons for the rejection.

Not only must the administrator maintain a sensitive environment for suggestions and new ideas, he must also be able to successfully convey final decisions to all members of the faculty. Occasional brief communications concerning work in progress can stimulate interest and encourage suggestions. By making everyone feel that he is part of the program, the administrator does much to insure its success.

Because of the number of decisions he must make, the administrator is more a generalist than a specialist and cannot afford time to study all specialities involved in program operation. He must be capable of rather quickly evaluating action programs presented to him by specialists, and he must insist on brief presentations containing basic facts if he is to be in a position to make decisions and to promote change.

Even when the administrator has carefully prepared the climate for change, he must expect considerable negative reaction. Many teachers feel uncomfortable when any new idea is tried, simply because it disturbs them to be shaken from their old ways. The administrator can hope only to keep obstructors to a minimum and then move ahead with those who are anxious to do so.

The administrator who initiates new programs and new facilities cannot afford to minimize the problem of financing them. Much of his energy and ingenuity will be devoted to allocating available funds wisely and cultivating the sources of revenue. Budgets tend to stabilize at some point, usually at the amount estimated as the maximum the voters will allow. If the program requires expenditures beyond this point, the administrator must convince the board of education and the voting public that a program is so essential it must be financed. His only other choice is the awkward procedure of cutting down on other services.

The concept of the IMC implies a great variety of services with more likely to evolve in the future. To say that the full potential of the IMC can be achieved immediately in all school districts, would be unreasonable. The administrator is faced with the problem of selection: he must plan programs and order materials according to relative worth and fit the selected services into the existing framework of his school or district. This selection of promising services and rejection of the least promising in the context of the individual school is one of the administrator's most vital and difficult jobs.

The administrator cannot extricate himself from the role of helping his teachers develop and synthesize a philosophy of education. Realizing that there will be differences of opinion, he will encourage enough consensus for cooperative action. The instructional media center is no exception. The staff must realize that the surface has hardly been scratched for improving methods of instruction and that we are in the business of constantly upgrading them.

The ability of an administrator to maintain a sense of purpose, a vision for the future, and even a willingness to risk bold action is most important. All other factors being equal, a faculty will follow a leader concerned with progressive change much more readily than one concerned only with the status quo. Naturally, such leadership must be accompanied with the ability to communicate and persuade in a non-threatening manner.

The Physical Setting

Although physical arrangements for the instructional media center are no more important than other factors, they cannot be ignored. Libraries during the past years have been characterized by inadequacies. Since the instructional media center should be a laboratory for learning, to be used by the entire school population, it is unacceptable for it to be so small that only a limited number of students can use it at a given time. Rather, it should be the central area of a building so conspicuous and attractive that no one can avoid it. Once the plans for a new building or remodeling of existing facilities have been accepted and bids for construction have been let, the die is cast.

Therefore, during the planning period, the administrator must do his work well. He must obtain all available information and use every method at his disposal to convince the policy makers of the need for adequate and flexible facilities.

The administrator, especially on the secondary school level, must depend on key personnel to work out details in planning physical facilities and must be alert to all suggestions from the staff. At the time when new buildings or additions to existing buildings are being considered, it is urgent that staff planning be initiated. The earliest stage of planning is the time to investigate all possible services to be incorporated in the instructional media center, to work out specifications, to investigate successful programs in other schools, and to scan the literature for ideas. Because so many of the ideas being incorporated in instructional media centers are still in a process of change and because sufficient time for evaluation has not yet elapsed, the job of planning becomes even more difficult. Far too many administrators take the easy road, accepting limited budgets without using proper persuasion and well-developed plans to convince boards of education. Lay people and boards of education are more responsive to new ideas than most people think, but they do not respond to hazy, poorly developed plans.

A great mass of new equipment has made selection difficult. Electronic devices, listening and viewing stations, tapes and records, study carrels, three-dimensional models, photography, transparencies, microfilm and teaching machines all bear considerable promise. Careful evaluation will show that many of these devices have already proven themselves useful, but limitations in budget always necessitate selections on the basis of priority needs. Selection and ordering of priority involve staff planning, not administrative mandate.

The Climate for Change

The principal's attitude and the steps he takes in setting the climate for change will be crucial to the success of any innovative program. He has a two-way task: to set the climate for change and to excite his subordinates and superiors as to the potential of the IMC. The following pattern of administrative action would be appropriate when a traditional library is to be changed to an instructional media center or when a new building is being planned.

1. Investigating the Proposal. The administrator must first investigate the nature and desirability of an IMC. An educational leader can hardly fail to realize its importance; however, if he is going to promote it effectively he must be thoroughly acquainted with its advantages and disadvantages.

Although the initiative for change is the responsibility of the administrator, the expertise for the IMC is likely to come from the library staff, probably the person in charge. These specialists, on his own staff or elsewhere, will be a primary source for the administrator familiarizing himself with the idea.

2. Developing Interest. If the administrator is convinced that the project is worthwhile, he must convince others and set the climate for change.

Although the IMC has broad implications for curriculum, explaining it to a skeptical faculty is far more difficult than any other part of the task. Failure to obtain faculty support will condemn an expensive, time-consuming project to failure, or at the very least, to mediocrity.

3. Setting up an Ad Hoc Committee. After a nucleus of faculty members has become interested in the project, an ad hoc committee should be appointed to study the project. Although the principal must be sure that certain interested and capable people will be present at the first meeting of the committee, he should invite all interested faculty members to attend. In making the first presentation, the principal can assert his concern and interest in the instructional media center, but the group should select its own leader. Although the principal can be rather positive in his interest, the committee's purpose at this point should be investigation and study. Arrangements should be made for reading the literature, assessing curricular needs, visiting instructional media centers, and seeking help from outside consultants. This stage may require considerable time depending upon the interest and know-how of the group. In the meantime, all members of the staff should receive periodic progress reports and be asked to make suggestions. Finally, the committee should report its findings to the administrator. If consensus on a program has been reached and the faculty in general is aware of this, a climate for change has begun.

4. Setting up a Permanent Committee. The climate for change should now be such that more rapid progress can be made. When the ad hoc committee finishes its preliminary investigation, permanent committees should tackle specific tasks and continue to communicate with and receive suggestions from the rest of the staff. If the climate

has been set, the group will be able to move toward a successful launching of the project.

Some administrators would expect the above procedure to be carried out in a shorter period of time with the administrator and the library staff doing most or all of the investigation. The slower procedure recommended here is based on the premise that an instructional media center is a total school project cutting across all curricular areas and, therefore, has little chance of success without a broad base of involvement.

5. School Board Approval. No administrator should move through steps one, two, three, and four without setting the stage for action with his superiors. Three points are essential in this relationship: regular progress reports by the principal to his superintendent and the board of education; mutual agreement on the administrative staff; open encouragement from the board of education.

The fact that a good instructional media center is more costly than a traditional library makes approval and understanding on the part of the board of education essential. Nothing is more defeating to the morale of an enthusiastic faculty than to have programs cut because of insufficient funds.

Implementation through Logical Persuasion

The instructional media center, as envisioned here, would bring about an extensive change in the learning process, but educators must not think of the IMC as a cure for all the ills and problems of education and as a substitute for good teachers. The learning process is extremely involved, and there can be no replacement for the good teacher. Some critics have expressed fears that the emotional elements of learning will be weakened as the more technical phases of instruction increase; that the central, directive influence of the teacher will be lost; and that the skills of the teacher to make use of the group process will diminish. Although there may be some cause for this concern, the results the critics foresee are not inevitable. The instructional media center with all its services must be used to serve the learning process, not dominate it.

Assuming that extensive outlays of money for the instructional media center will meet with resistance from those who control budgets, as well as by those who resist change for other reasons, the administrator must clearly formulate arguments he can use for its promotion. He will at the same time be formulating goals for it to fulfill. These arguments can readily be supported by the rationale listed below.

1. Increased Motivation. The topic of motivation has been much emphasized in recent years. Motivation as a process in education is difficult to define. The mere mention of it makes some people see red. All people do not agree on the responsibility of the school for motivating students, claiming that educators have sometimes sought a level of motivation that is impossible to attain. All of us are aware of distinct limitations on the extent to which instruction can overcome environmental and genetic factors. However, the function of education is to change people, and without the assumption that good teaching and well-organized programs can change attitudes, no success is possible.

The instructional media center can be a powerful force in increasing the motivational level of students. Classroom instruction limited to basic textbooks becomes boring to many students. The opportunity to explore freely in an attractive learning laboratory and to experience the exciting process of investigation for knowledge can provide

The IMC can increase the motivational level of students

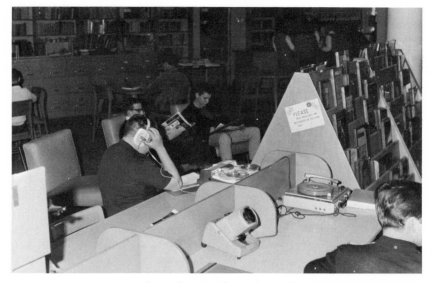

Independent Study in the IMC

much more interest than traditional methods. For example, one of the most interesting possibilities provided by programmed learning is that some students who have been mentally blocked and unable to progress satisfactorily by means of traditional methods may be able to learn in a prescribed, logical manner. The current success of the language laboratory with its individualized instruction also tends to bear out this hope. Thus, a variety of approaches to learning, including independent study in the IMC, can reasonably be expected to intensify the desire of students to learn.

2. Antidote for Overcoming the Weaknesses of Mass Education. Up to the present time, instruction in the typical classroom has been primarily a group process. Although considerable provision has been made for individual pursuits of learning, lockstep procedures still compel every child to cover the same unit of study or even the same pages in a textbook. By and large, the pace has been set for the average learner with little provision for those in the group who are either slower or more gifted. Many leading educators have pointed out that a high percentage of gifted students remain unmotivated and never seriously enter into the learning process. A similar concern can be shown for those less capable. Since many learnings are sequential in nature, a failure to attain parts of the sequence prevents future learnings.

When the instructional media center is accepted and used in the instructional programs, it can help remove this problem. Recently developed programs in independent study have been quite successful. Through this method, capable students are released from classroom discussions and drill they no longer need and can move into exciting areas of exploratory study. However, such programs cannot be unstructured. The classroom teacher, the consultants in the instructional media center, and the student must plan as a team to develop this program.

When a student learns the skills of investigation, he possesses the ability to learn on his own initiative with a minimum of help from others. This skill is vital for any mature person and can be attained, at least to some degree, by most children.

3. The Development of Skills. By the time students reach the freshman year of the secondary school, great differences within grade levels appear in all divisions of the curriculum. This is especially evident in skill development. Reading, spelling, computation, and the ability to communicate orally and in writing are all relative attainments. Even the most capable students are able to improve skill development when given the right environment. The norms for skill development become higher each year, because of better instruction on the elementary school level, but modern society demands an ever-increas-

Areas of Exploratory Study in the IMC

ing level of proficiency. The child who reads or communicates below his grade level is severely handicapped.

The instructional media center can play a vital role in skill development. A strong argument can be made for a skills laboratory in every school: students must have an opportunity to sharpen the basic skills under capable teachers who encourage them to help themselves as they improve their ability to read, spell, write, prepare talks, and do basic mathematics. Such skills laboratories should contain listening posts, viewing stations, recording booths, study carrels, teaching machines, typing facilities, collected materials for units of study, provisions of reading improvement, and other appropriate learning areas. It seems obvious that the skills laboratory should be an integral part of the instructional media center. Many teachers are likely to see the value of the skills laboratory and will come to appreciate the full scope of the IMC more readily from this starting point.

4. Increasing the Rate of Maturation of Students. By the end of the twelfth grade, a student abruptly leaves the protection of home and school and becomes largely responsible for his own success or failure. There is much reason to believe that both the home and the school have been reluctant to accept and to meet the challenge of preparing for this change in the student's life. The three or four years of high school should be years of increasing maturity; responsibility and ability to function alone should develop along with social and academic proficiency. From this perspective, the educator can present a strong argument for the instructional media center with its provisions for independent study, skill development, and freedom to pursue knowledge and areas of interest. There is a strong rationale for increased attention to faster maturation of students. A senior should be more psychologically oriented toward self-sufficiency than a freshman. The instructional media center will help orient him, but only if it is more than physical space with learning equipment. The student must be made aware of the need for independent study and learn self-responsibility for skill development. He should visualize his entrance into a less directed and less protected period of his life and see that he must prepare himself accordingly.

Teacher Involvement

In the early planning stages, the attention of the faculty must be focused on the more pragmatic expectations of the instructional media center. However, the problem of implementation of the program is still to be faced. As previously mentioned, teacher participation in the use of the instructional media center is most vital and difficult. The high degree of departmentalization in high schools has often served as a deterrent to the use of special services. Key personnel, such as department chairmen, can make or break a program. Departments have a strong tendency to set up facilities within their own curricular areas for convenience and ease of operation and are often passive toward total school operations. However, this passivity can result from the failure of centralized services to meet the challenge of their operations because of inadequate physical facilities and/or inadequate staff.

The practice of departments' setting up centers of their own for instructional materials is basically inefficient. First, this arrangement causes an expensive duplication of facilities; and second, teachers are too busy and, in most cases, inadequately trained to make use of the complex media found in typical IMCs without expensive consultant help. On this premise, administrators must find a way to involve teachers on a total school basis, or even a total district level, if efficiency is to be attained.

Basic to the successful involvement of teachers in this mode of instruction are the following:

1. Physical Setting and Staff Adequacy. The IMC must be adequate from the standpoint of both facilities and staff. However, it is far better to temporarily limit facilities than to do things poorly. A successful experience for teachers in the use of instructional media is the best way to gain confidence and a desire for needed services.

2. Staff and Faculty Cooperation. Ideas for the use of media must not be limited to IMC staff members. Classroom teachers have much to offer. Conversely, whenever a teacher needs films, tapes, records, or prepared materials, the IMC staff should respond quickly and with enthusiasm.

3. Improved Teacher Education. Colleges will have to emphasize the importance of instructional materials in teacher education. Coordination between library schools and colleges of education has improved considerably, but continued effort is essential. One aspect of a teacher's education should be the use of facilities. How can a teacher appreciate and make full use of the tools of learning unless he has been personally involved? As new techniques appear, education must not merely keep up; it must serve as the cutting edge. Colleges of ed-

ucation should not be intimidated into neglecting the improvement of instructional methods by critics who think that anyone who knows a subject discipline can teach. Teaching, like all other professions, requires skill in method of operation along with proficiency in knowledge of subject matter.

4. In-Service Education Programs. In-service programs are becoming more and more essential. If the cliche "teaching is an art" means that teachers have innate creativeness or that they automatically acquire it through academic pursuits, it is not enough. Admittedly, potential teachers have certain aptitudes and gain much from subject matter and studies in the liberal arts, but they need to learn how to teach and to make efficient use of all media and methods. Continuing programs of teacher education are invaluable and are most successful when they take place in the school. On-the-job consultants can show teachers how to make use of transparencies, and how to use audiovisual techniques and the most recent electronic equipment. Teachers also need to learn how to find materials in the IMC.

The instructional media center must depend on the classroom teacher when new materials are selected for purchase each year. In-service programs should familiarize teachers with the multitude of materials available and enable each curricular area to evaluate its tools of learning.

5. Curriculum Study. The administration of the school should assume positive leadership in setting up provisions for curriculum study. Failure to do so tends to negate any possibility for positive change. Workshops and time within the school day for in-service work are essential. Unfortunately, many schools make little provision for this vital work; too often they go along from day to day with each department and each teacher working separately and having little knowledge of what is going on in other parts of the school. This serious problem needs correction.

6. Student Involvement. Student use of IMC facilities is fundamental. Many teachers make assignments in such a way as to create motivation for use of the center; others make textbook assignments and entirely avoid involvement of students in the instructional center. The teacher's attitude will usually determine the extent of student use. Teacher involvement in the establishment of an IMC again proves to be a critical factor.

Provisions must be made to train students to use the IMC efficiently. This skill is somewhat complex and does not occur by accident. Students will seldom become involved in the use of facilities without a planned program. A unit of study should help inform pupils about what is available as well as the techniques of usage. This unit of study must be more than a tour of the center or lectures by staff members. The student must learn how to check out materials, the techniques of reporting after having listened to records, the use of reference materials, and so on. An interesting, well-planned center attracts students. Once there, they should be given the opportunity to browse and explore for their own satisfaction in a place where a multitude of materials are readily available.

The classroom teacher's role in the successful operation of the instructional media center makes him indispensable. He must be depended upon to set up classroom plans that will guarantee its use. No amount of coaxing from administration or the IMC staff will be successful unless the teacher is convinced that the IMC has value. The interested teacher must be trained by the specialists in the center. Perhaps with patient effort, the prevailing tendency to use a single textbook can be overcome.

Staffing the Instructional Media Center

The many services an IMC can offer in addition to library and audiovisual services complicate the problem of adequate staffing. The American Library Association in 1960 recommended one librarian per 300 students for the first 900 students, with an increase of 50 percent where audiovisual services are incorporated in the library. One clerk for each 600 students plus an additional 50 percent for audiovisual services was deemed necessary.[1] The new standards recommend one full-time specialist for every 251 students, or major fraction thereof.[2] They further recommend at least one media technician and one media aide be employed for each media specialist.[3] Specific staffing recommendations were also given in the 1960 standards for the new school[4] and the small school with less than 200 students.[5]

The present shortage of librarians, to say nothing of directors of IMCs, is even more complex qualitatively than quantitatively. The image of the old-fashioned librarian is a far cry from the professionally trained consultant working effectively in an IMC. One encouraging element, however, is that skilled clerks can do much more than was originally believed. Under the direction of professional staff

members, they learn readily and can relieve the staff for more important duties.

Salaries for adequate staff plus the expense for all types of instructional materials is far greater than most budgets now allow. Increased
responsibility of library clerks can cut down the overall expenditure
of an adequate staff, although the ALA recommends that, because of
their specialized skills, library clerks be differentiated in the salary
scale from other clerical workers. Although the matter of budgets cannot be developed at length here, it must not be taken lightly.

The Director of the IMC

Not only must the IMC have an adequate number of staff members,
but their training must be of high quality. This is especially true of
the director of the IMC. "A statement prepared by the Joint AASL-
ACRL-DAVI Committee" outlines the professional prerequisites of
the instructional media specialist:

1. *Successful teaching experience:* . . . years of classroom teaching
or . . . an organized internship program. . . . It is essential that instructional materials specialists secure experience on curriculum committees and that they gain experience in guidance and supervision.

2. *Foundation areas:* Instructional materials specialists should have
course work in (a) educational administration and supervision, (b)
principles of learning, (c) curriculum development, (d) guidance and
counseling, and (e) mass communications. Furthermore, they should
demonstrate a working knowledge of research methods as applied to
instructional materials.

3. *Specialized areas:* Instructional materials specialists should have
course work and in-service experience in . . . (a) analysis of instructional materials, their nature and content; (b) methods of selecting
and evaluating materials, through study of individual media as well
as through cross-media study by curriculum unit or grade level; (c)
utilization of materials; (d) production of appropriate instructional
materials, including laboratory work with specific media; and (e) processes for the organization and maintenance of materials and equipment.[6]

In addition to his training, there are other qualifications that the school administrator should seek in appointing a director of an instructional media center.

1. He should be highly creative and sensitive to ideas and new concepts. His vision will enable a school to develop a sensitivity toward new movements that bear promise and to reject the ones that are inopportune.

2. He must possess the somewhat rare ability to influence others. The fact that he is an expert must not prevent him from working cooperatively with his staff and faculty. His power of persuasion, backed by his training, enthusiasm, and boundless energy, will cause others to follow. He will be continually influencing administrators, his own staff members, and fellow teachers, and in a sense will serve as a catalyst for change.

3. His philosophy of service must set a tone for the instructional media center. The image of the librarian as a "keeper of the books" is caused by the negative aspects of the duties involved, but it is well known that some personalities are more successful than others in setting healthy climates in libraries and instructional media centers. The IMC must be a pleasant place, and the director will definitely establish the atmosphere.

4. He must be able to function in groups. His role at times will be very similar to that of a curriculum coordinator. In this setting he must be able to listen to others, injecting his professional opinion into the planning, but never engineering his point of view at the expense of others. He will understand that a high degree of involvement on the part of the faculty is so important that consensus on planning must be attained even at the risk of some loss along other lines.

5. He must not become devastated by plans and ideas that fail to develop. Good leaders have always been able to sustain temporary disappointments and then rise and return to the battle. He will think in terms of percentage of improvement, instead of pinning all his hopes on one issue.

Finding a director with these qualifications is definitely a problem, but is no different from staffing in other parts of the school. As goals become clearer and preparation more careful, sufficient people of this order will emerge. A previous part of this chapter has dealt with "setting the climate." It must be assumed that those in leadership positions will give the director the type of support which will enable him to assume the type of role we seek. Good directors will be anxious to work in schools with good climates and have already shown that they are quite selective as to where they work.

Administrators who would promote the implementation of instructional media centers must realize that:

1. they are costly in time, effort and money;
2. they possess deep curricular implications;
3. their use will, in many cases, be opposed by some who resist change.

However, they are well worth the time, effort, and financial outlay needed for their success. As educators move toward improved instruction, the IMC will undoubtedly play a leading role. It may be the forerunner of a new era in education in which better instruction will be a prime concern and will be entered into with enthusiasm and concerted effort. IMCs are not cure-alls, but they are essential if better methods of instruction are to be found.

PART III

IMCs IN ACTION

CHAPTER 9

An Elementary School IMC

by

ORVILLE JENKINS

As principal of Moreland Elementary School, Shaker Heights, Ohio, Orville J. Jenkins directed a program which attracted visitors from surrounding states, the West, and Canada. He had had experience as a sixth grade teacher in Mentor and Maumee, Ohio, and as a supervising teacher and principal in Bowling Green, Ohio.

Mr. Jenkins held an M.Ed. degree from Bowling Green State University and was working toward an Ed.D. at Western Reserve University prior to his untimely death from cancer. Among his published articles are "Why Team Teaching?" in Scholastic Teacher *and "Team Teaching and the Intern" in* Ohio Schools.

The School

MORELAND ELEMENTARY SCHOOL, located in Shaker Heights, Ohio, a suburb contiguous to Cleveland, is an integrated school serving many children who have arrived within the past three years from the inner city. Twenty-four classroom teachers, a full-time IMC teacher, an IMC aide, specialists in French, physical education, speech, art, vocal and instrumental music, a reading teacher, a principal, two secretaries, an adjustment teacher, a co-op worker, five custodians, an instructional assistant, several student teachers each quarter, a social worker, a psychologist, a nurse, and several volunteer workers make up the staff.

Constructed 45 years ago, Moreland is an old school—a school de-

scribed in district literature as "an imposing brick structure with tall
Ionic columns dominating the front of the building situated somewhat
forbiddingly atop a terraced hillside, a school which gives off an air
of formality, dignity and a kind of classical self-assurance. The exterior may be forbidding, but the interior is inviting. It is a school
whose corridors and rooms demonstrate a vitality—it is a place
where exciting things happen daily."

As our neighborhood changed and our school became integrated,
we met new problems with a vigorous approach. Recognizing that the
traditional middle-class approach to education was no longer adequate to meet our needs, we changed the school. Today we have a
program designed for kids rather than teachers. Playing a major part
in this approach is our learning center or IMC.

The Beginning

The concept of the instructional media center took shape in Shaker
Heights in 1962 when two of its schools, Lomond and Ludlow, were
involved in a Ford Foundation project to convert their libraries into
learning centers. Additional personnel, study carrels, library stacks,
and listening and viewing areas were made available to these two
schools. Prior to that time, our libraries housed primarily books and
magazines.

Year by year, all the libraries added more nonprint media. Each
school library received a master console unit and a listening-viewing
panel. Gradually, individual IMCs were established in all the schools.
In most instances, these were apart but close by the libraries. New insights into the teaching-learning process were gained. A stronger
commitment to a multimedia, multisensory approach to learning developed. A coordinator of teaching media was employed and the district's first teaching media center was born.

Today that district center is housed in Moreland Elementary and
serves the centers of all 12 schools in the district. More than 14,000
books each year are ordered and processed in this central department. The coordinator of this center holds monthly meetings with all
librarians, wherein 100 to 150 new books are reviewed, common
problems discussed, and plans made for improving the IMCs.

The teaching media center for the district hums with activity. The
coordinator sets up in-service workshops in all the buildings for

teachers, children, and interested parents. He and his graphic arts technician work in the schools to develop individual centers where materials are created. In our school, for example, the instructional aides and volunteer workers produce transparencies, dry mount and laminate materials, and replenish self-instructional materials as needed.

The district center sends out to the schools master films, copies of master tapes, and numerous kits and models. Transparencies are created upon request. The work of this department serves to strengthen all the IMCs in the district by sending out printed and nonprinted materials to enhance the instructional programs. New equipment, new films, and new techniques in the use of audiovisual materials are introduced continuously to the schools.

Each elementary school IMC in the district works within a budget which provides $4.05 per child for materials. Moreland, for example, will have approximately $2,300 to spend in a one-year period.

Our Center

Despite this centralized program, each school IMC has the freedom to develop in its own way. One school may invest heavily in books, while another leans toward nonprint media. Similarly, each school IMC has a unique appearance adapted to its own facilities. Unfortunately, our IMC is smaller than we would wish. In the future, we hope to add an adjacent classroom to our IMC and thus provide additional service. At present we have approximately 11,000 books, 30 periodicals, 650 filmstrips, 250 records, 75 tapes, and many, many pictures and pamphlets.

Four to eight volunteers from the community and 35 to 40 upper grade children work under the guidance of the librarian. They assist in processing books and other nonprinted media and assist with circulation and reference work. Upon entering the IMC, one sees fluorescent lighting, acoustical tile ceiling, study carrels, displays of children's art work, and open shelves of filmstrips, records, and tapes. A closer look reveals a sofa and a carpeted area, where children may sit while reading or listening to a story. A viewing and listening area with a master console—record changer, two tape decks, and controls —provides another set of learning experiences for children. Individually operated volume and channel controls and electrical outlets for

The viewing and listening area provides learning experiences for students.

plugging in filmstrip viewers or film projectors are located along one wall.

The picture file, a magazine rack displaying many different magazines for both children and staff, tables with seating facilities for 42 children, a micro-projector, small screens, several filmstrip viewers, a 16mm projector, a globe, an 8mm film-loop projector, a pull-down screen, bookcases arranged in stacks, and a book-drop are framed by eight windows which look out on many trees, bushes, and shrubs. The view is striking throughout the year.

Our Philosophy

What makes an IMC important is how it is used. Here is where Moreland's IMC is different. We have a philosophy about children in which we believe. For example, we dislike the phrase "at the close of school." If instruction is truly individualized, school will not end at a magic hour. Each child will have an individual closing time which will vary from day to day. Let me illustrate.

DING! DING! DONG! "Hey, kids! Have you seen the film, "Down Under?" It's terrific. It's in color. It tells the story of the exciting, colorful life under the sea. It shows a new world of life, of food, of adventure, and of beauty. Come to the IMC at the close of school today to see it. You may also see it tomorrow morning at 8:30. You'll like it."

That was Camille, one of our sixth graders, talking to our 580 children over the intercom. She is a promoter, a salesman, and an announcer. Her enthusiastic endorsement of the film brought many children to the IMC at 3:15, where they put on headphones and viewed the 16mm film, thereby extending their horizons and forming new concepts.

We believe films are exciting for children, helping to transfer enthusiasm into the field of reading. In this effort to upgrade reading skills and to develop a love for reading, we use a variety of techniques. Upper grade children read to primary children. The librarian, teachers, and volunteers tell stories and read to the children individually and in small groups. They team up weekly to plan specific IMC events and activities. Reading and learning messages bounce through-

Films can transfer enthusiasm into the field of reading.

out the school in signs, announcements, skits, bulletins, and programs involving children and staff.

Films and filmstrips concerning books, authors, and book publishing are shown by the teachers, who also speak often to small groups of parents about the value of books in the home, how to help children become better readers, and the relation of reading to personal development.

Someday we hope to eliminate the stodgy term "librarian" and replace it with the more meaningful title "IMC Teacher." We want children to see her as a teacher who facilitates learning, not as a custodian of books.

A lively tenet of our philosophy is that education cannot be confined to classroom-curriculum activities. It must spill over and saturate the building. We try to involve every individual in the school. Children are encouraged to help each other. Some study alone, in pairs, or in small groups. Some work in individual study carrels; others lie on a carpeted section of floor reading to themselves or to others. The IMC teacher, in cooperation with the staff, constantly strives to strengthen children's research skills and to broaden children's interests.

We Involve Parents

Change wasn't easy. It took hard work. Limited staff, personnel changes, tradition, lack of space, and a growing student population have plagued our efforts, but we still managed to make progress and have never felt discouraged.

One way in which we promoted change was by involving parents. We tried to keep them informed every step of the way and to enlist their help as volunteer workers for the school. An example follows.

A MESSAGE TO THE COMMUNITY

Dear Parents:

It is good periodically to look backwards to see how far we have come since the opening of school. It is equally good to then gaze into the future to see where we are headed. There are plans to discuss with you soon the past, present, and future of Moreland. This paper will serve as a springboard to additional "Parents in Conversation" small group meetings with staff members joining in, to both our February and March PTA meetings, and to a planned dialogue experience at the school. Parents and the school will together work on various problems which could well have some positive benefits for all our children in this year and the years ahead. Your feedback concerning the program at Moreland is needed; your greater involvement in the program at Moreland is urged. Your ideas, criticism, and encouragement bounced up against our ideas, criticism, and encouragement (for you) will fall out into something better for your child.

Now, look over your shoulder. . . . Children and parents received at their houses a personalized form of class assignment before school started. This was just the beginning of many new innovations and exciting events. . . . Many parents helped to get supplies to children during the first few days of school. . . . There was a new feeling of enthusiasm in the air. . . . You could feel it and you could see it by observing classroom happenings. This still continues. A sparkling group of teachers were at work creating an environment in which your children could work most effectively. . . . There was then and there continues to be now a questioning attitude throughout the community related to the advantages and disadvantages of a predominately Negro school. People have lined up on both sides of the question while others ride the fence. . . . There need to be more opportunities for open discussion about this difficult issue. Talk costs nothing and can be very productive.

Moreland P.I.P. came into being. A "Personalized Instructional Program" began to take shape with the ungrading of the primary grades. Eleven teachers began to talk of ways to individualize instruction—to make possible daily success for every child—to concern themselves more with human values. . . . Grades on a competitive basis were changed to grades on an individual basis. New reading materials were introduced into classrooms. . . . More children were involved in listening experiences with headphones and tape recorders. . . . Children could view films before and after school in the learning center. . . . Classes were of different sizes as different children were grouped for different reasons. . . . Unique seating arrangements began to appear in the classrooms. . . . Initial Teaching Alphabet (i.t.a.) was introduced in two of our kindergarten classes. . . . An all-boys' class with a male teacher was started. . . . Total involvement and problem-solving activities were introduced in our physical education program. Children have certainly responded to this with enthusiasm. . . . Approximately 20 volunteer workers were assigned to work with individual children. This program is proving to be successful. . . . Some of our sixth graders work with individual primary grade children before and after school to help them with certain skills. Children are able to help other children learn. . . . Five Byron Junior High girls are working with five fifth grade girls once a week after school in math. . . . A chess club is a going thing. . . . Different weekly newspapers are in 20 of our 24 classrooms in consideration of the different reading abilities. . . . A sports club has been organized for fifth grade boys and girls with the emphasis on gymnastics. . . . Sixth grade boys meet after school each Tuesday and Friday to play basketball.

Many different groups of people from other parts of Shaker Heights have been invited in to see Moreland in action. The Rotary Club, the Master Plan Advisory Committee, the PTA presidents and vice-presidents, ten members from the Housing office, and a group of parents from another elementary school have had this opportunity. It is fair to say that the majority of these people have been thrilled with what they have seen—and well they might. The quality of instruction in this building is excellent. We have high-achieving children who are being challenged, and we have children who have real difficulty reading, spelling, and writing. We are providing them with much help. As might be expected, we are having more success with some than with others.

The large majority of our children are well-dressed, well-behaved boys and girls. There are only a few children in this building who are in trouble repeatedly. We haven't found the answer to this problem as yet, but we will before long. Discipline as such is not a major problem in this school. Good teaching is responsible for this.

What about tomorrow? There will be after-school basketball for girls, more family film nights, much, much more individualized teaching, classes of children of different ages, a greater variety of teaching materials in the classroom, a paperback bookstore, more opportunities for some children to engage in independent study, many more small-group activities, more special-interest groups, a different math program for different children, the entire school ungraded, more involvement of parents, greater emphasis on the creative arts, extended use of tape recorders and headphones, improved reading materials, improved guidance and counseling, and more contact with other schools.

We are presently planning to bring some of our children together with children from other buildings for different experiences.

More attention will be given to communication skills and to thinking. School will be more relevant to more boys and girls. Each child will feel completely accepted—as he is. Human values will be given a position of even greater importance.

Teachers will be assuming greater responsibility in designing programs to meet every child's needs. We already know that every child who fails in school will probably fail in life. We can't permit this to happen. Many adjustments will be made to insure success for more and more children. Dreams? Yes, but only as we dream can we make significant progress. We expect much because of the great progress we have already made. There is no limit to the future improvement of our school. Your children deserve the best we have to offer. That's what they are getting today; that's what they will be getting tomorrow. We are learning—will continue to learn—how to work with individual children. It's demanding and frustrating at times—but very exciting and stimulating. It's what education is all about. It takes great teachers with deep commitment. There is no choice. It's a race between survival and chaos for the individual child.

Education is everybody's business. It's important business. It deserves that all-out effort from parents, children, and educators.

Moreland today is better than it has ever been. You have reason to feel real pride in its accomplishments. It is deeply concerned about every child in the building. It makes mistakes but it moves forward. Whatever tomorrow brings, Moreland will continue to do its best for every child who comes in its doors.

By the way, we could use your help at school. Call us and volunteer your services for children.

THE PRINCIPAL

Do these communiques work? They seem to. Our parents and teachers are informed, and lines of communication are open. Many parents willingly work in the school and help in a variety of ways.

Volunteers in the IMC

Assignments vary depending on the interests and abilities of the volunteers. Some work on a regularly scheduled basis and others as time

A volunteer reads to children.

permits. They serve both children and staff. They update the card catalog file, place books on shelves, assist boys and girls in locating materials, read with individual children, and dry mount and laminate pictures. They also organize and catalog tapes, records, pictures, and filmstrips. What a huge effort this is! Thank goodness for volunteer helpers.

AN INTERVIEW WITH A VOLUNTEER

Asked to give her opinion concerning work in the center, one of the mothers who volunteers reported as follows:

> I love the school environment. I would rather be in school than out bowling. I feel I am helping my child as well as the librarian and the teachers. The work is very satisfying to me. I like to know in advance what I'm going to do when I come in to work. I prefer working with books or the card catalog file. I am impressed with the individual learning which goes on in the IMC. Children are given more consideration and more help with their individual problems now that classes have been unscheduled. The instruction was too impersonal before. The children seem to enjoy coming in to look around, to read, or to do research. They seem more self-sufficient. The librarian is also free to help individual children.

A continuous effort has been made to interpret the school to the parents, to involve the school in the community, to involve parents in their school, and to build a stronger, more positive image of the school throughout the broader Shaker Heights community. The following is a list of projects, activities, and programs which have either been tried recently or are presently in effect in an effort to develop a community school:

1. an evening Open House in the spring for children and parents;
2. principal's newsletter, PTA newsletter, classroom newsletters, school newspaper, and a Community Association newsletter;
3. "Quiz the Principal" meetings;
4. Curriculum Fairs;
5. Outdoor Children's Art Show on Memorial Day co-sponsored by Community Association, PTA, and the school;
6. activity clubs for children in embroidery, chess, dramatics, and knitting;
7. Father-Son nights in the gym;
8. a breakfast for fathers prepared by the school staff;
9. joint PTA–School skits;
10. volunteer services for teachers and children provided by mothers;
11. education parties throughout the community (teachers and parents);
12. "Parents-in-Conversation" program—many small groups meeting throughout the community discussing education at Moreland;
13. Block Club dinner for staff;
14. seminars in creative reading, creative art, creative music, and creative dramatics for parents;
15. family film nights;
16. family-style hootenanny, International Food Fair, square dance, art workshop, and talent show;
17. corn roast—family style;
18. Teachers' Appreciation Night Banquet;
19. after-school basketball for sixth grade boys;
20. after-school basketball and volleyball for sixth grade girls;
21. staff luncheons twice a year served by parents;
22. grade-level evening programs involving children and parents;
23. Children's Youth Corps established to develop pride in neighborhood through litter campaign, anti-sidewalk writing, and anti-fighting campaign;

24. attitude survey every other year;

25. Negro history seminars held by mothers;

26. work with the Community Association on many projects involving youth.

All of these programs have helped us build a bridge into our community. We have succeeded mightily in developing within the community a sense of pride in the school. There is, however, a need for a continuous effort in this regard. New families continue to move into our neighborhood. There are too many families who haven't been reached as yet.

Time for Independent Study

As indicated in the message to parents, several classes were involved in an experiment with unscheduled time. There was a general feeling that greater flexibility was needed in the IMC to meet individual children's needs. After much discussion, a plan was devised which included orientation of children and parents on procedures for checking books in and out, and for using IMC materials on an individual basis. Records were kept of the use being made of all materials. The results of an end-of-the-year evaluation were overwhelmingly in favor of con-

The IMC is available throughout the day.

tinuing the new program. Children, teachers, and parents indicated a strong interest in the individual approach.

Early in the 1967–68 school year, the IMC teacher structured grade-level meetings for further discussion on the use of the IMC. Following an orientation period, the staff decided to unschedule the upper grades and to begin a gradual unscheduling of the primary classes. The objectives were well defined, and the program worked. We were interested in providing individual help for all children, giving them additional opportunities to select their own materials. We were interested in having the IMC teacher available throughout the day to work with individuals and small groups of children.

The IMC and the Nongraded Primary

Thirteen classroom teachers, including two kindergarten teachers, work as a primary team along with the reading teacher, five student teachers, and an instructional assistant. One of these teachers is designated a unit leader. There are four division leaders. Individual and group conferences with the IMC teacher are held often to coordinate learning activities and to discuss learning materials which will enhance the continuous progress concept for each of the 280 children.

There are large- and small-group activities as well as independent inquiry experiences. Children are encouraged to program their own learning activities, and self-instruction materials are available upon prescription. Children complete many learning tasks at their own learning rates. The IMC teacher makes an effort to know something about each child's interests and abilities. She and the classroom teacher, together with the reading teacher and other specialists as needed, confer about various children's progress. They also work together to help each child with his reading program—skill development, attitudes, and recreational reading. Specific materials are ordered upon the recommendation of one or more of these teachers.

The primary grade children are now able to find their way around the IMC. Some said it couldn't be done, but these children now select their own books from the shelves, using shirt cardboards to mark the places from which they pull their books. This system permits them to browse and to choose from many books and magazines which interest them. Previously, the children could select only from a few books pulled from the shelves and put on the tables.

Student Aides

A particularly interesting aspect of this primary program is the help given by intermediate grade pupils. Selected upper grade children are assigned to tutor primary grade children before and after school and even during the school day. Under the guidance of the classroom teachers, these tutors ably assist in the areas of perception and motor skill development. They often read with their "charges." They handle the book checkout, thus saving teachers' time and energy. These student helpers also learn to operate A-V equipment and show films throughout the day. Their enthusiasm is infectious and helps to spread a love for learning.

Although emphasis is placed on reading in the primary grades, the IMC program broadens as children mature. All fourth graders receive instruction in the use of the card catalog file, how to find various materials, and the use of various reference books. Some children, on more of an individualized basis, are introduced to these in the upper primary grades. We provide this type of instruction to children in groups of five on an intensive basis. One of our volunteer workers, a former librarian, assists. The results are excellent.

To spread enthusiasm, children are encouraged to talk over the intercom about the books they are reading. This excites other children's interests and, of course, enables the speakers to share their personal enjoyment. They prepare their own announcements, often with the assistance of the IMC teacher, who encourages an informal approach. Here is just one example of how our IMC teacher also promotes use of the IMC over the P.A. system:

> DING! DING! DONG! Good morning, kids! Starting tomorrow, there will be a special display outside the "IMC" of new books, records, filmstrips, and tapes. Come on down and browse any time you are free during the next two days. Listen in this afternoon for the DOO-BEE-DONG SINGERS. They have some new songs they want to sing to you about the IMC.

It wouldn't be fair to imply that the use of children as IMC aides has been an unqualified success. We have problems, too. The boys who run the film projector occasionally forget to show up when it is time to show a film. —— A few teachers just can't seem to "free" their children very often to work in the IMC. —— Sometimes the filmstrips get into the wrong containers. —— We forget at times that children require time to browse and we hurry them. —— At times it gets a bit noisy in the IMC. Our kids like to talk. —— Some of our children don't bring their books back on time. —— On occasion, not too often, discipline problems are sent to the IMC to read—or at least they are sent out of their rooms. They seem to do OK at this, so maybe it isn't such a bad idea. —— Maybe we overencouraged a couple of teachers to send children to the center to work. They sent some of their "charges" in with pasting and crayoning work. Perhaps our job now is to fill up those seats with boys and girls doing legitimate research and study so those with the crayons can't find a place to work. Despite these problems, the gains make the program well worth the effort.

Teachers' Meetings

The IMC teacher often schedules noon-hour sessions for the staff in the IMC, where they not only eat, talk, and socialize but accomplish quite a bit. They thrash out problems, trade ideas, and make decisions which usually benefit the children. As a result of these meetings, teachers take an increasing interest in the IMC and assume more responsibility for its operation and for resolving some of its problems. It was at such a meeting that we developed the plan for our paperback bookshop.

The Bookshop

The bookshop committee consisted of the librarian, the IMC teacher, and a primary teacher. Our bookshop is a portable case opening up into two large sections which hold 100 paperbacks. A local agency supplied it for us.

A week-long paperback book sale in our own Doo-Bee-Dong Shop was highly successful, with 245 books sold. Individually selected, the books covered such subjects as cooking, housekeeping, gardening, grooming, poetry, baby and child care, and sewing. Some biographies and novels were included. Each child received a bookplate and wrapping paper at the time of purchase. We sold more than 1,000 paperbacks during the year. We went out of doors with the shop on

Memorial Day for our annual Children's May Art Show and sold over $40 worth of books.

Pupils learned that there are many books which can help all of us do things better. Perhaps more importantly, they thought of their mothers as "readers." Ten children had the experience of working in the shop handling money, keeping records, and helping younger children make their book selections.

Messages to the Staff

SPECIAL BULLETIN—RE: OPENING OF SCHOOL

We surely seem to be off to an excellent start. Our materials, equipment, and books are adequate, and our class sizes are quite good. Our physical plant gives us room for most of our activities.

Your interest in providing your children with a first-rate educational program is evident. On the whole, there is a mighty fine spirit running through the building.

Our children come to us in all sizes, with varying abilities, and with different degrees of interest. Each child is ours to teach—to help to the best of our ability. Different learning styles on the part of some children demand different teaching styles on our part. Our own attitudes play a most significant part in our effectiveness. Do we possess those important qualities of warmth, friendliness, and fairness? Do we relate positively to every child? Unless we do, we will fail some child.

Every child needs to feel that we have faith in him. Our actions will tell him whether we do or not.

Every child needs to be held to a high set of standards. We must not settle for less than a child's best. Extend and challenge each child day by day through a continuous set of successful learning experiences. This calls for great teaching—inspirational teaching. We are capable of that.

It calls for strong, positive feelings of pride in this school. If we don't have that we don't have anything. This comes only through a united, cooperative team approach, creative teaching, a great desire to help children, and a willingness to change from outmoded, worn-out practices which actually prevent children from learning.

The image of this building is ours to make. What it is now is what we have made it.

Each staff member has an important role in helping all our parents to have confidence in this school. Each of us has a job to do in helping each child to have respect for his school.

One of our major objectives certainly must be that of motivating each child to do his best. This calls for strength (firmness and self-confidence), for clear thinking, for a wise use of materials, time, and space. Work that is too easy, anything but challenging, brings loss of interest, apathy, and trouble. Work that is handed out daily in the same packages with large amounts of "teacher talk," warnings, threats, and admonishments without regard for the individual will too often bring negative results.

Work that is stimulating, that involves each child, that is nonthreatening, that is accompanied by a relaxed atmosphere, encouragement, and a sense of humor will bring desired results.

The way we talk about children tells something about the way we feel about them. Destructive comments don't belong in any school. A professional approach to our work calls for insight, understanding, empathy, personal care, and diagnosis. Each child has dignity, and it is for us to respect it.

Discipline? This word means different things to different people. Without it, there will be chaos. With it, but without the strong humanizing elements, there will be grimness. In between these two extremes is that place where we want to be—where order prevails within an atmosphere of aliveness, where each child is encouraged and accepted. Mistakes lead toward improvement rather than more frustration. It should be legal, quite acceptable, to make mistakes in every classroom.

Plays, skits, trips, projects involving construction, imaginative uses of books and nonprinted materials, films, tapes, and homework of a creative nature belong in every classroom.

This is a school—an excellent school, a friendly school. This is the school which will give you as much if not more than you give it. From what I have observed so far, we have everything we need to make this the best year yet.

A Staff Memo: What a School!

What a school this could be if every staff member responded to the challenges positively. What a school this could be if everyone, all of us, were interested in sharing ideas, in learning from each other, in supporting each other, in sharing in each other's successes and fail-ures. What a school this could be if everyone assumed some responsi-bility in solving certain problems. What a school this could be if everyone considered himself a learner. What a school this could be if everyone were truly professional. Come to think of it, we aren't too far away from this utopia.

What a school this is! There are solid reasons why I and many oth-ers are proud to be here serving our children and our families. There are many excellent teachers on this staff—many professionals who are positive in their actions, who care enough about children to go that extra mile willingly. There are many staff members who work well with their colleagues rather than working in competition with them.

What a school this is! Many exciting things are happening in our classrooms. Problems are being solved; children are learning. Every-one can take credit for this. A major breakthrough is being made in the area of individualized instruction. Hard work? Of course! Some-one must pioneer, though. Someone must care enough to want to make education more relevant to every child. Someone must make this massive effort in order that ample materials, equipment, and staff can be made available.

Everyone can find a dozen reasons why it is impossible to individu-alize instruction. Anyone can say, "It can't be done! It takes too much time." Yes, of course, it is demanding, but we're fortunate to have people on this staff who are willing to make that big effort—who are doing it. We are individualizing instruction in many classrooms—in varying degrees, in different ways, with different approaches. Every type of effort is needed. Every person's ideas are needed. Much shar-ing and conversing should be taking place. Many questions should be asked. Inquiry is needed.

To the extent that not enough inquiry is going on, we should see that this is corrected. People of "good will" will take care of this problem.

To the extent that misunderstandings and competitive feelings have developed which close off communication, we should move to correct this by engaging grade levels in dialogue, by bringing about greater exchange of thoughts at the "Honest and Open" level. People of good will, of good faith, can do this—and people of good will we have in abundance. Within the near future, such small-group meetings will be structured.

We have no race going to see who can individualize the best or the fastest. We do have a big commitment to the concept involved. We do have a need for more dreaming—for more people to say "I can and I will." Dreams can be realized right here today—and they will be. It only takes some imagination, some desire to improve, some strong feeling that what you are doing is not good enough, some belief in your ability to make a significant difference in children's lives, some conviction to an idea. Translate this dream onto paper and let's see what will happen.

What a school! Something is happening! People are dreaming! People are thinking and arguing, frustrated and elated, disappointed and encouraged, angry and happy, disturbed and on fire. This is the way progress is made. This is the way we are. This is good. The ingredients for pulling through any storm are all here.

There are those staff members who are already feeling some concern about poor communication between some individuals and grade levels and who want to do something about it. This is encouraging. There are many staff members who continue to work together, share ideas together—and this is terrific. All of us need to pull in this direction. We will! We have sufficient staff leadership—all over the place.

This is everybody's business. This is our school. Everyone must see himself as a decision-maker.

What a school! Ideas are being born. Education is becoming more relevant. Excitement is in the air.

We can help each other by remembering each of us is only one. Each of us has a contribution to make. Each contribution needs to be accepted. Children will benefit as we continue to do away with practices that frustrate, as we continue to look to ourselves for answers rather than to blame children because they don't always meet our standards or our expectations.

What a school! What a staff! What an opportunity we have!

Teachers Speak Up

Teachers seem to like our nongraded team approach. They enjoy the flexibility of unscheduled time and are learning to use it in advantageous ways. Here is what a few have to say.

Fran (Grade 6): "It has been most helpful to have the IMC available any time during the day. Children were able to work there on open-ended assignments. We used it, too, for recreational reading. One group used the center for long hours in examining different sets of reference books available in relation to difficulty, quantity and quality of information, pictures, charts, maps, and graphs."

Karen (Primary): "We have greatly enjoyed having the IMC unscheduled. My children like to work there independently. We have used the center frequently recently in our study of reference books. I like the flexibility."

Ethel (Grade 5): "Different children alternated between my room and the IMC as a part of an individualized reading program. All children used the center many times for research. Individual experiments in science were performed as a result of some of these trips. We borrowed pictures for room displays and recordings related to our social studies units."

Mickey (Primary): "I hope to use the IMC more next year. I sent children periodically to the IMC to work independently at the study carrels."

Ruth (Grade 6): "The resources and potential of the IMC are tremendous. I plan a new approach for the coming year with many more children working there."

The Future

Our fine IMC will continue to evolve—will continue to serve people, to strengthen the teaching-learning process throughout the school. It will become even more of a hub of learning—a focal point in a school where individualized instruction is a major thrust.

Our supply of nonprinted materials must be increased substantially. The appearance of the center will be improved with new draperies and child-centered furnishings. A greater use of color would help. Soft, more comfortable chairs are desirable. We will continue to dream about having carpeting throughout the center. Some solid thinking will go into increasing the size of the center to provide more moving around space for children to engage in a variety of learning experiences. Additional staff would help immensely. This will come eventually, we hope. A media specialist would move us ahead considerably. Videotaping is upon us now, and more and more programmed materials are appearing on the market. We will take advantage of these materials in due time, particularly since we have a videotape recorder as a result of Title I funds. Creative thought and energy will be required to move our learning center into a true instructional media center. In the words of a visitor who spent some time with us recently: "Overall, there is a spirit of youth and excitement at Moreland School. From the humming lower-level art center to the second-floor classrooms with their novel seating arrangements, the spirit is pervasive and contagious. Behind the imposing facade of Greek columns and the terraced front lawn, an exciting challenge to tired concepts of dull education is daily and joyously being flung."

Inasmuch as our school is involved in many innovations in an attempt at improving the quality of our education, it is imperative that we keep in close touch with our parents and our community. Now is the time to involve our total community and our school in an even more meaningful dialogue and planned program directed at improving human relations and providing new opportunities for personal development. We have some children who need much, much help with their educational as well as emotional problems. We must develop a stronger program in working with their parents.

Our dreams are many. Our potential for realizing more and more of these dreams is great. Our need to realize these dreams is based upon the great "American Dream" of providing quality education for every man's child. Parents and teachers, home and school, must clasp hands regularly within an atmosphere of mutual respect and trust if children are to receive the fullest benefits from their education. The school must be a vital force within its community.

CHAPTER 10

A Junior High School IMC

by

LEILA A. DOYLE

Currently the consultant for school library services in the Gary Public Schools, Gary, Indiana, Leila A. Doyle has had experience in the elementary and secondary schools in Gary and at Purdue and Ball State universities. She earned her M.S. degree at Indiana University and did her undergraduate work at New York State University.

Miss Doyle's professional responsibilities include serving on the Board of Directors for the American Association of School Librarians and on the American Library Association Council and acting as consultant on instructional media projects. The latter included the Title II Project—State of Nebraska.

SCHOOL MEDIA CENTERS are essential to quality education. But the mere fact of having centers, beautiful and well equipped though they may be, will not ensure this kind of education. There are at least two additional essential elements: first, that the school have as its objective to teach children how to think—how to organize their work, analyze problems, and seek solutions, thereby sharpening their mental processes; and second, that the center be staffed with qualified, creative professional personnel, and highly skilled technical and clerical personnel. The professional staff must be knowledgeable about the objectives of education, striving to improve methods of teaching and searching for more effective and efficient ways to create an environment for learning. Staff members must be provided in sufficient num-

147

bers for the media centers to ensure full educational return from the wealth of materials available.

Writing for the *PTA Magazine,* Nancy Larrick, a well-known authority in the reading field, commented on the access we now have to a rich variety of teaching aids, and added: "The final test is how these teaching materials are used. The school that furnishes eight workbooks for each second grader and no library books is spending lavishly for intellectual poverty." [1] Miss Larrick also referred to the deterrent lockstep effect created by the single text.

There is a difference between imparting information and helping children to read and to think for themselves. The latter does not necessarily follow the former. Educators today place far greater emphasis on self-education which will continue the process of learning throughout life, than on instruction which may terminate at the end of formal schooling.

We in the media area are concerned with the education of all children. The function of the library media program is to help teachers do a better job of teaching and to help boys and girls do a better job of learning. The integrated curriculum of today requires that both pupils and teachers have access to a wide variety of instructional materials: books, films, filmstrips, globes, maps, pamphlets, periodicals, pictures, realia, recordings, transparencies, slides, stereographs, and so on. Radio and television are also important instructional tools. The use of textbooks alone, regardless of their worth, does not suffice and can no longer be considered adequate as a medium of instruction. Teachers are becoming increasingly aware of the need to employ a wide variety of materials and media to meet the range in abilities, interests, and needs of boys and girls. The aims of good teaching are to enrich the curriculum, to challenge the developing mind, and to inspire to greater achievement. It is clearly evident that the educational effort is directed toward developing sound critical thinking based on carefully formed judgments.

It is of utmost importance that we keep in mind our ultimate educational goals as we discuss library media centers—their materials, organization, and program of services. Media centers exist for one purpose—the education of children. Therefore, in the "Handbook" for our Gary Public School Media Centers we state that our purpose in teaching a pupil is to help him grow in self-direction. The focus is on individualization of learning, for which the center is designed. Even more than this, we are dedicated to enriching the lives of children and stretching their horizons.

Background

The Gary Public Schools had centralized elementary and high school libraries more than 40 years ago. They were originally organized on a unit plan with children from grades one through 12 housed in one building. Each school building had two centralized libraries, one serving the kindergarten through grade eight, the other serving grades nine through 12. The program for audiovisual services was a very early development, growing out of the auditorium program. With the increase of available instructional materials and equipment and the emphasis on the use of these aids to instruction in the classroom, some of the school libraries expanded their programs to include the newer media (1940). Where this was not done, due to limited space or conventional attitudes, an audiovisual department was organized within the school. At the same time, changes in the organizational pattern of the schools resulted in the elimination of the auditorium program as it was then known. As the need for additional classrooms grew, elementary schools were designed for the kindergarten through grade six. The first major building program undertaken by the Gary schools since the construction of original unit buildings did not include quarters for centralized library services. When the results of this omission became evident, future plans for elementary schools included the media center. All schools now have centralized media centers: The 34 elementary and six secondary schools have completely integrated programs; the remaining 11 secondary schools are in various stages of integrating and coordinating their programs. The present building program provides for additions to the older buildings. These will include centers with space and facilities for the complete program of instructional media services. To date it has been the philosophy of the personnel in the media area to build a firm foundation for excellence in all schools rather than to provide superior services in one school while others trail behind. The Gary school librarians believe that a consistent organizational pattern for all the media centers is in the best interest of the teachers, students, and media staff. Children move from elementary to junior to senior high schools, and from schools in one area of the city to another. There is also mobility among the teachers; therefore, a standard organizational pattern is designed to facilitate this transition from one school and one area to another.

Too, the library media centers in the individual schools are served by a centralized technical service area, which is assuming an ever-increasing workload by expanding its services in the processing of instructional media. The services currently provided by the technical service area include:

Acquisitions. All requests are received and processed in this center.

Cataloging. The Dewey decimal classification system is used for all materials. (Although there are advantages in using other systems for some materials, we believe that the consistency provided far outweighs the disadvantages). Shelflist and catalog cards are prepared.

Processing. Initially only books were processed, but this service is now extended to filmstrips and phono-discs. It will soon include all instructional materials acquired for media centers, whatever their form.

The schools are also served by a centralized educational film library with over 3,400 titles, an equipment repair area, and various other related services.

The technical service area has established a color-code system for the various materials, which is standard for all the centers:

Books, Circulating	White shelflist card Red edged catalog cards White circulation card
Books, Reference	White shelflist card Orange edged catalog cards Orange circulation card
Filmstrips	White shelflist card White catalog card with green edge Green circulation card
Slides	White shelflist card White catalog card with green edge Green circulation card
Equipment	White shelflist card White catalog card with blue edge Blue circulation card
Phono-discs	White shelflist card White catalog card with buff edge Buff circulation card

Tapes	White shelflist card White catalog card with black edge Buff circulation card
Kits	White shelflist card White catalog card with plain edge White circulation card
Specimens	White shelflist card White catalog card with purple edge White circulation card
Transparencies	White shelflist card White catalog card with orange edge White circulation card
Picture sets	White shelflist card White catalog card with brown edge White circulation card
Periodicals	Cherry circulation card

For Title II materials, banded shelflist cards are used for quick identification when they are interfiled with the shelflist cards for other materials.

Shelflist cards, Title II:	Red banded	1965–66
	Green banded	1966–67
	Blue banded	1967–68
	Black banded	1968–69

The services provided by the technical service area determine, in part, the organizational pattern of the individual school center. However, the staff time saved in not having to process books is now spent in making selections and ordering additional instructional materials. This is because of a material budget which has more than doubled and over $300,000 in Title II E.S.E.A. P.L. 89-10 funds.

Bailly Media Center

Two new identical junior high schools were constructed in Gary at the same time, Bailly and Beckman. These centers received identical furnishings and equipment. The Bailly Media Center was designed to make possible a centralized facility where the books, audiovisual materials, and equipment would be organized and made easily accessible to teachers and students—where the center could, in fact, become the laboratory of the school, an extension of each classroom. The facilities include a reading room seating 80 students, with viewing and listening areas in the main room. Four separate rooms opening into the reading room serve as office, workroom-preparation area, equipment storage, and professional room, with a folding wall providing for one or two conference rooms as needed. The area is attractive in appearance. The wall shelving is supplemented by counter height shelving, which forms area divisions. As the room has considerable natural light, both the floors and walls are in pastel shades. The furniture is walnut finish. Work areas for the students are provided by square and round reading tables, each seating four, and 10 individual study tables. A Readers' Guide table equipped with filmstrip viewers provides a carrel. If we were to select furniture today, we would increase the number of individual study tables and request a second Readers' Guide table.

When the Bailly and Beckman Media Centers were originally

Viewers are always in use, and the filmstrips are shelved nearby in the Bailly Junior High School Library Materials Center, Gary, Indiana.

Individuals or groups use earphones to listen to phono-discs and
tapes in the Bailly Junior High School IMC.

planned, provision was made for a folding wall between the work
and office areas to provide for group use of materials and equipment.
In the final plans this item was omitted, as were many of the electrical outlets. Carpeting was also requested, but we were a year too
early! Since these two junior high schools were opened, carpeting has
been the accepted floor covering for all new media center installa-
tions. There were disappointments, but the advantages provided by
these new quarters far outweighed the disadvantages. The administrators, the faculty, and the students were as enthusiastic as the staff
of the media center in their desire to develop an effective program
and to create an atmosphere conducive to learning.

Each book, periodical, pamphlet, filmstrip, phono-disc, model, puzzle, and each item of equipment for the Bailly Media Center was selected with knowledge of the curriculum and the interests, needs, and
abilities of junior high school pupils. There was a wide range of
printed and audiovisual materials to take young people beyond the
limits of the classroom in every subject area, and to fill individual
needs. Consideration was given to the range of reading abilities,
which became wider in each successive grade level. We chose the

best of our literary heritage to take children into the world of imagination and fantasy. Children, at times more than adults, need release
from their tensions and problems.

Organization

The card catalog in the media center is an index to all the varied materials in the collection. Interfiling the cards for all materials makes
the user aware of the many materials available on a given subject.
The catalog also indexes the 16mm films owned by the school system.
A student making a study of Brazil may find books on the history, geography, travel, and biography of that country; books with individual
chapters covering art and government; fiction books with Brazilian
settings; phono-discs presenting the folklore and music; study prints;
pictorial maps; filmstrips and films.

Careful organization of materials and equipment is important. The
system should provide for as consistent a pattern as is feasible for the
location of needed materials, whether they are in print, on film,
taped, or in other form. It must provide for a circulation system that
is easily understood and operated and furnishes the kinds of information needed in evaluating the collection. The organization should also
make possible the maintaining of accurate business reports. As ours is
a liberal circulation policy, there are book pockets and charging
cards in all reference books. The orange circulation cards indicate
that the book is limited to overnight circulation. Older issues may be
charged out for a week.

After discussing the use of copy and accession numbers, we decided to stamp books, circulation cards, and shelflist cards with a
numbering machine and to eliminate entry in an accession record
book. Experience had shown that far more errors are made in both
entering copy numbers and in the carding of books when copy numbers are used. Children make a minimum of errors in the "carding" of
books when they are taught to check the accession number.

Models, filmstrips, phono-discs, and picture sets are circulated like
books. All are cataloged centrally. The filmstrips arrive in the media
center with the shelflist, catalog and green circulation cards, and a
typed label on the container. Adding the call number to the inside
area at the end of the strip is an excellent idea, as it provides a means
for checking to see if the filmstrip is in its proper container. Gaylord

filmstrip boxes are used so that the filmstrips can be shelved in Dewey order.

Phono-discs arrive in the school center with the label attached to the center of the disc, accompanied by shelflist, catalog, and buff circulation cards. We use plastic jackets with pockets, making the typing and pasting of pockets unnecessary. We insert labels in the upper left-hand corner of the plastic jacket, and shelve the phono-discs in Dewey order. No accession record book is kept for books, filmstrips, or phono-discs.

Frequently, models, jigsaw puzzle maps, pictorial maps, picture sets and study prints, and other instructional materials are purchased from lesser known sources. Maintaining an accession record of these acquisitions provides a permanent record of the source and price. Circulation cards are provided for all these materials. When pockets cannot be attached, the circulation card is filed at the charging desk.

Each item of equipment is also entered in an accession record book. This provides a permanent record of entry date, model, and length of service. It will also, in time, afford information relative to the "life" and use of the equipment. Since there should be an accounting for public funds expended, these records will provide a reference

Educational games are popular with the children.

for source and cost. The equipment is labeled with the name of the school media center, serial number, and accession number. Blue circulation cards and book pockets are typed with the accession number used as "call number," and pockets are attached to the bulletin board in the equipment storage room. The circulation procedure is the same as that used for books and other materials.

When materials and equipment are centralized, those that were selected for a particular subject area are available to all teachers and pupils. For example, a model of the ear, ostensibly for science, may be regularly used by the speech teacher and the speech and hearing therapist. Microscopic slides and the microscope may be used in the library by a child who is not in a science class. In fact, there are few instructional materials which are used exclusively by one department. Most materials may be checked out for home use.

Program

The purpose of education is to teach children how to think, to investigate, to search out facts, and to evaluate. From the very earliest years in schools, children must learn to question and to consult a variety of sources. Can they verify the information contained in filmstrips or films? Are there other points of view? In developing children's tremendous potential for learning, we cannot begin too early to capitalize on their natural curiosity. It is from this premise that the program for the media center was developed at Bailly.

At the opening of school each year all seventh grade classes participate in an orientation program in the center, where they are introduced to the many kinds of materials and their locations. They learn the procedures used in borrowing materials and the opportunities they will have to use these resources. We give a minimum of instruction at this time, as details are more meaningful when presented in connection with reference projects, which require specific knowledge and skill.

Teachers and librarians together plan for classes, groups, and individuals to use the center as their laboratory. Students are given guidance in exploring the resources, making selections, and developing creative projects. Working on one project may include the use of printed and audiovisual materials; the use of the opaque projector to enlarge and copy an illustration; and the use of the tape recorder in preparing a report. Provision is made for students to work alone or in groups. The research for another project may require only the use of specialized reference books. An attempt is made to tailor the program to the needs, giving the students an opportunity to explore.

Although the elements of a good program are present, we must also note the shortcomings. We cannot meet the demand for services, particularly the work with children in the center, because of limited staff. Two full-time paraprofessional people are needed; we have only one half-time secretary. Three professional media specialists are needed; we have only two. The program has grown beyond our ability to meet the needs and requests.

Reading

Reading has not diminished in importance with the advent of other media. In fact, there is greater emphasis on reading than ever before. There is only one reason for a child to learn to read; and that is *to read*. He must find satisfaction and enjoyment in reading if he is to become a reader.

Yes, we read books too!

Although stimulation, encouragement, and guidance in reading are given in all phases of the media program, children need individual guidance if they are to grow in their reading habits and tastes. Teachers and librarians work together to provide time and opportunity for work with individual children; however, this all-important function will be fully realized only when sufficient school library staff is available.

Services to Classrooms

The excellent library of 16mm educational films is maintained in the school service center for all the Gary Public Schools. In Bailly the teachers request these films through the media center. Knowing the films requested affords the media staff another opportunity to give additional services. A few well-selected books, study prints, or other materials related to the subject of the films are sent to the classroom with the film and projector. Sometimes these are accompanied by a note suggesting additional materials or services the teacher may wish to use.

Collections of books are checked out to the classroom. Although all books are available for use in the classroom, special reference books are usually borrowed for a limited time. If the demand for a particular reference book is great, duplicates are ordered so that one copy is always available in the center. Filmstrips and recordings may be scheduled in advance or obtained on a moment's notice. Again, duplicate copies are obtained when needed.

Other services to the classrooms are:

Picture sets, models, display materials—in fact, any materials the library has—are circulated to the classroom.

Equipment is furnished for use in classrooms. Selected students from each class are given very careful training as projectionists. Teachers also are trained so they may supervise the student projectionist or operate the equipment in an emergency.

The library staff prepares reading lists, source lists, and bibliographies in cooperation with the teachers.

Transparencies are obtained from commercial sources or prepared in the center as requested by teachers.

Educational radio programs are taped so they may be used when needed.

The dry mount press is available for use by teachers or student assistants.

The professional library area, which adjoins the media center, affords teachers a private library in which to work. Communication between the media center staff and classroom teachers is greatly improved when teachers are easily accessible. The program of the school IMC is determined largely by the educational philosophy held by teachers and the methods of teaching, which are an expression of this philosophy. Most teachers recognize that textbooks are chrono-

Pictures and study prints are used by children as well as teachers.

logical or topical outlines; they are guides. The Bailly teachers plan their classroom activities and assignments so the children become involved in seeking information, in gathering data, and in evaluating their findings. They seek to extend the educational experiences—not limit them. When this happens, the best use is made of the library resources and personnel, and education of a quality not otherwise possible is available.

The Bailly Junior High School Media Center is not able to give all the services requested. But with the administrators, teachers, and media staff working to achieve excellence in their educational program for children, continuous progress will be made toward this goal.

CHAPTER 11

A Senior High School IMC

by

JEAN ELAINE WICHERS

Jean Elaine Wichers is an assistant professor of librarianship at San Jose State College, San Jose, California. Prior to 1965 she served as librarian on all levels in various public schools in California.

Mrs. Wichers has a B.S. degree from Kansas State University and an M.A. from San Jose State College. Among the periodicals to which she contributes are California School Libraries *and* Audio-Visual Instruction. *She frequently addresses district workshops on such topics as instructional media and the changing role of the school librarian.*

SEASIDE HIGH SCHOOL is a comprehensive American high school. Peopled by boys and girls of varying races and varying religions, it is about as all-American an institution as one can find anywhere. Student attitudes are wholesome and positive in relation to each other, making it a most rewarding and challenging place to work. Most scores on IQ and achievement tests cluster around the 50th percentile. The staff median age is 35 and averages seven and one-half years of teaching experience. About half of the teachers have earned their M.A. degree.

Seaside High School serves an area which includes Fort Ord, a large infantry training base, the city of Marina, and an estimated 50 percent of Seaside, California. Most of Seaside's income is derived from the military base and from the resort and tourist trade attracted by its location in the world-famed Monterey Peninsula. Approximately 60 to 65 percent of the parents are connected with the military, and 40 to 45 percent live on Fort Ord. Although this presents the school with the problem of a largely mobile group of students, it also has a plus factor. Having spent much of their lives overseas, these students have had experiences that enrich the activities of the entire school.

The Dream Materializes

A dozen years ago, Seaside High School was only a dream. In 1959 as a new high school was being considered in the Monterey School District, an educational planning commission was formed. This group, called "The Citizens Advisory Committee," met with the Board of Trustees of the district, the administrative staff, and representative teachers to develop plans for the new school.

It had been 40 years since the Monterey District had built a new high school. Therefore, the community showed keen interest in the endeavor as they planned the very best for their young people. Realizing that advances in technology as well as changing patterns in learning and teaching demanded new stress on individualized instruction and independent study, it was agreed an instructional media center was needed.

The IMC Concept Is Realized

At that time the idea of a high school instructional media center was in the beginning stages of realization on a national scale. Traditional libraries were often storehouses of books, carefully guarded and little used. The educational planning commission, as well as the teachers and administrators of Monterey, had the foresight and vision to see the advantages of the multimedia concept in teaching and learning. By September 1960, plans for the Seaside High School, including the IMC, were approved by the Board of Trustees.

From its inception, the instructional media center was regarded as the "heart of the school." Accompanied by members of an architectural firm on Monterey, the steering committee visited high schools all over California. In an effort to combine the best features of each, they talked with teachers, librarians, administrators, and, most important, students. They learned from what they saw; they designed the

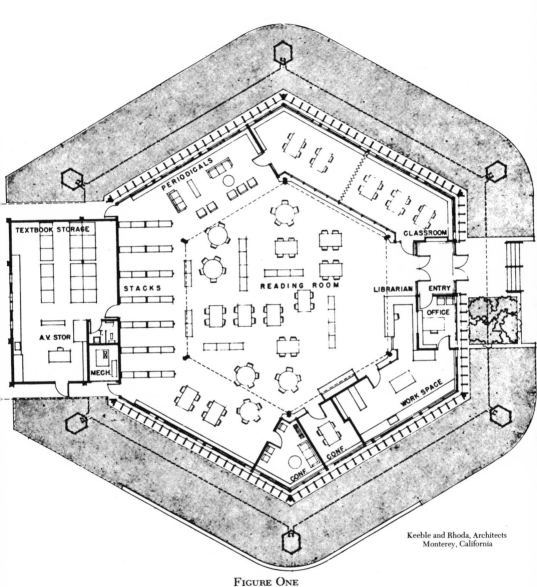

Keeble and Rhoda, Architects
Monterey, California

FIGURE ONE
SEASIDE HIGH SCHOOL LIBRARY FLOOR PLAN

IMC in the geographical center of the school plant. This strategic location was to be a prime requisite in the total design. Other requisites were expandability, attractiveness, good lighting, and open access to materials. A hexagonal design provided peripheral advantages in that the main reading room was surrounded by a classroom area for library skills instruction, conference rooms for small-group discussion, a professional reading room for the faculty, a workroom, and the librarian's office. The textbook room was located beyond the open shelves of the main book collection.

The Materials Collection

Understanding that the link between a sound curriculum and its effective implementation rests upon good teaching practice and proper instructional materials, the staff designed an exemplary collection at Seaside High School. Concepts emerging on the educational scene involved programmed instruction, team teaching, flexible scheduling, independent study, and discovery and inquiry methods of teaching. These concepts provided a broad base for the selection process. Selection of the library collection was made within the framework of a sound district policy. Materials included books, magazines, newspapers, documents, programmed materials, flat pictures, study prints, vertical file materials, pamphlets, bulletins, recordings, audiotapes, discs, maps, globes, graphs, charts, diagrams, posters, listening and language laboratories, reference materials, and encyclopedias.

Capital outlay funds provided by the Board of Trustees one year before the school was to be in operation made it possible to secure books, equipment, and materials in advance. Six projects, providing matching funds from the National Defense Education Act, made it possible to have outstanding materials in specific disciplines such as mathematics, English, and foreign language. Standard book selection tools were used as directives in the acquisition of the materials. The American Library Association's *Basic Book Collection for Senior High Schools* was ordered almost in its entirety.

The media center was well stocked and functioning on the opening day of school. This was one of the most important factors leading to its success. Students learned immediately that this was a different library. Here was their learning resource center, filled with materials they could use, with a librarian eager to help them, in an atmosphere beyond their expectations. It was a warm, friendly place to study.

Physical Facilities of the Center

The location of the building is ideal. It is the focal point of architectural composition and student attention. To minimize distraction and to enhance the beauty of the exterior, there is a grade separation with a large area of attractive plantings. Vertical precast fins placed at two-foot intervals around the IMC keep it from becoming a "fishbowl" and add beauty to the design of the building.

The interior space is organized around a central reading room with auxiliary areas and conference rooms on the perimeter. Acoustical

Exterior view of the Seaside High School Instructional Materials Center, Monterey Peninsula Unified School District, California.

Students working on a committee project in the Seaside High School Instructional Material Center.

plaster ceiling finish and "tactum" wallboards on the upper portion of walls combine with carpeted floors to reduce noise. Six-foot circular, recessed fluorescent lights around the perimeter and light fixtures arranged in a sunburst design in the domed ceiling provide excellent light. Moreover, the arrangement creates a most sensitive response from all who enter the library. The instructional media center was awarded the National Award of Merit for Design Excellence by the American Institute of Architects and the American Library Association in April 1964.

There are three exits and a door leading to the textbook and equipment room. The vestibule entry is carpeted with a vinyl resilient floor covering which is highly resistant to sand and dirt. This is critically important because the school is built on land with a sandy composition. The entire reading area is carpeted with nylon floor covering. This has proved to be well worth the investment when maintenance and esthetic factors are considered. Students respond favorably to the quiet atmosphere afforded by carpeting and find the environment conducive to quiet study.

"The Proof of the Pudding"

The many hours of planning that involved the principal, the architect, the steering committee, the district staff, the librarian, department chairmen, and teachers were rewarded in a sense of achievement on the opening of school as the students walked into the IMC. Pupils found a well-stocked, well-organized, and functioning center. They were able to borrow materials the first day of school. The importance of having a media center ready for circulation at the opening of school cannot be overemphasized in establishing the proper tone and spirit for student acceptance.

"The heart of a school" is not a new phrase for an instructional media center. At Seaside High School it is meant sincerely by the faculty, the students, and the community. They share a pride in their IMC and strive to keep it functioning efficiently.

Description of the Instructional Media Center

At the beginning of each school year, the librarian encourages the teachers to make use of the resources housed in the center. This includes the books, periodicals, pamphlet files, and nonbook materials and equipment. The center is a learning laboratory where students may learn at their own pace, according to their own interests. It is a key area for each teacher, who can, with the help of the librarian, use the resource materials, the conference areas, and the reference sections to enrich classroom activities. Teachers are encouraged to bring classes to the IMC and to suggest materials for the librarian to add.

The hexagon-shaped design has lived up to its goal. The classroom within the walls of the library provides countless opportunities for instruction. Acoustics make the room ideal for a lecture-type situation, leaving the reading room free for independent study. Students often attend lectures in the conference room and then pursue individual reading. With proper organization, the demands of the schedule can be met to allow teachers plenty of library participation.

The furniture in the instructional media center was chosen because of its beauty of design and sturdiness. A variety of round and rectan-

This classroom in the Seaside High School Instructional Materials Center is used for library skills instruction and special classroom conferences.

gular tables, naugahyde-upholstered armchairs, and straight chairs provide a general atmosphere of comfort, beauty, and strength. Students appreciate the fact that typewriters are available as part of the IMC service. Pupils often use them to prepare assignments for classes, to copy necessary information from books, and to practice typing skills.

Open stacks house the library book collection. Books are charged out from the main charging desk located near the entrance to the library. Reference materials and periodicals are shelved in areas around the perimeter of the reading room. Current periodicals are displayed in plastic binders on slanted shelving adjacent to the newspaper racks. Comfortable armchairs are arranged around magazine tables for reading and browsing.

A microfilm reader-printer precludes the need to store more than the minimal amount of periodical literature. The need for actual magazines still exists, but the microfilm library provides a beginning library with out-of-date materials otherwise impossible to obtain. By combining the back issues of periodicals with the microfilm reels of specific titles used in the various departments, such as the social sci-

Librarian charging materials from the Seaside High School Instructional Material Center.

ence department's request for a historical coverage of the Civil War period or the Victorian Era, a library can provide optimum learning resources.

Another Exemplary Center

Besides the Seaside High School Instructional Media Center, many high school IMCs contain ideas worthy of emulation, though only one other example can be described here. A pioneer in educational communications is the Oak Park and River Forest High School in Oak Park, Illinois. The primary objective is the same as Seaside's: to help the students learn better; to help the teachers teach better.

Located west of Chicago, this high school, with more than 3,700 students enrolled, serves a residential area quite unlike the Seaside community. The school was established in 1875. There is no industry in the residential villages, and the per pupil cost is one of the highest in the country. In contrast to the transient enrollment at Seaside, Oak Park residents cherish the fact that they have many "two- or three-generation families" among the graduates. The school atmosphere is steeped in tradition. Some of the regulations have remained the same for 50 years. Great importance is attached to the collection of books written by former students of the school, which includes technical and creative works.

The high school library program has long been built on the instructional materials and multimedia concept. It enjoys the reputation of being selected by the American Library Association as a national library demonstration center. It provides reference, reading, and listening facilities to all its students. It exemplifes the media center that serves as a true extension of the classroom as it enriches the curriculum and strengthens each teacher's program with its abundant materials collection. At the present time this collection contains more than 45,000 books, 270 periodicals, 1,200 filmstrips, almost 600 films, 1,200 recordings, 945 transparencies, 3,500 slides, over 500 microfilm reels, and 900 retrieval tapes.

The library personnel has always demonstrated an unusually warm and friendly attitude of helpfulness and service. There is provision for formal class instruction in the use of the library, fortified with individual guidance as the students request materials. There are many sources of programmed instruction, realia, and exhibit materials available to every department of the school.

Students using a random access system.

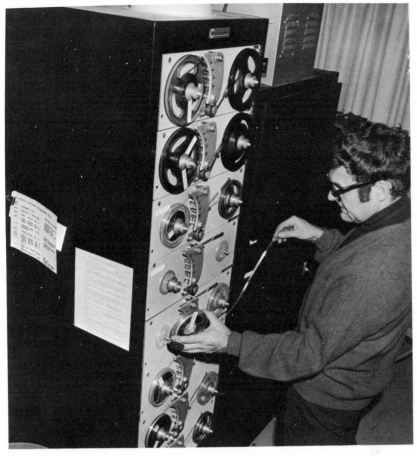

Loading a tape deck for a dial-select audio system.

The new audio system is the first true random access audio information retrieval system in any high school in the United States. Random access is a method of storing programs and data by which any item can be brought forth immediately. It can be called a true random access system because each student in any of 25 different locations can select from 224 recorded programs and have his selection available for listening in his own earphones in less than 59 seconds. Program length can be up to 15 minutes long, a maximum length for the average attention span when an Oak Park student is learning by repetitive presentation.

Through funds made possible by a federal grant, a larger bank of programs and carrels for viewing is being installed. The library retrieval project personnel think that the random access method can meet the needs of the majority of students. This includes the highly motivated ones who need to go beyond the reaches of the average, the poorly motivated ones who need individual help to overcome a lack of concern, and the bulk of other students, who for many reasons find that this method of learning "works."

Special Library Reading Rooms

Forty years ago an American history reading room was established in the Oak Park and River Forest High School. It has become one of many such reading rooms. An art library is housed in the midst of the art department facility. Portfolios, reference sources on the history of art, and techniques and theories within the art discipline are readily available whenever the student needs them. Located between the language laboratories and the foreign language classroom is the foreign language library. The professional librarian is a former foreign language teacher who, along with the rest of the professional library staff, divides his schedule between the main reading room and the special reading room. The new mathematics and science library is located near the physics laboratories.

These special reading and study areas have been given various labels. Since the appearance of "sputnik," educators have called them "satellite libraries." Providing easy access to special collections, they attempt to bring materials and users closer together. In some schools, there have been occasions when such satellite libraries did not achieve their purpose. This happened when no personnel from the library staff was assigned to that specific reading room. Hence, the materials soon became out of sequence, lost, or unused. Sometimes departmental libraries failed because there was little or no communication between the central IMC and the department. As school campuses increase in size, it is feasible to maintain successful satellite libraries within a high school plant. However, this will happen only when there is good communication between the faculty, the library staff, and the students using these special reading rooms. As is the case at Oak Park, the entire IMC operation requires adequate staff, materials, and facilities. At Oak Park, the present IMC staff includes four librarians, two A-V specialists, two half-time librarians, seven half-time library aides, and three clerical secretaries.

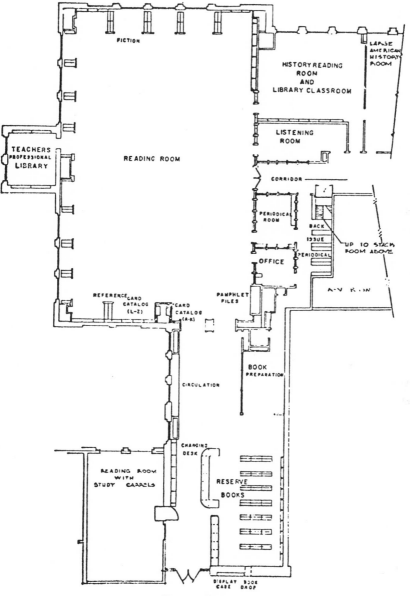

FIGURE TWO
THE OAK PARK AND RIVER FOREST HIGH SCHOOL LIBRARY

Teachers and Librarians with a Common Goal

The effectiveness of the Oak Park and River Forest High School IMC program is largely due to the cooperation between the library staff and the faculty. The curriculum must be designed to incorporate learning resources. The library staff must inform the teachers of its holdings. Here, a great deal of time is spent on the preparation of bibliographies. Special materials are borrowed from neighboring libraries through interlibrary loans. Public libraries are kept abreast of current and future projects so they may be prepared for requests. Teachers are encouraged to suggest materials to be ordered.

Oak Park has found that the elementary and junior high schools must be involved in good library instruction. This articulation between the levels of learning is one of the prime requisites when a school strives to achieve a total learning experience for its young people. The elementary school student who establishes good study habits takes the work in his stride as he progresses to junior and senior high school. He uses the instructional media center instinctively. New books, new media, new techniques are as much a part of his school day as are his teachers.

Application of Technology and Media

A high school is a conglomerate, ever-moving community of ideas, bodies, and images. It is a place where mass media and people meet; a place where communication takes place. The role of the educator in a high school becomes crucial in determining communication behavior. The administrator of the instructional media center, with his staff of professional librarians, media specialists, clerks, and secretaries, plays a key role in the secondary school drama.

Whether the school is relatively new like Seaside or well-established like the Oak Park and River Forest High School near metropolitan Chicago, the needs of the young people remain much the same. They have individual desires and abilities. They strive to achieve at their own rates. Their future will be determined by the habits they acquire in their early years. This includes the use of learning materials.

Applications of technology and new media in all subject areas demand that the instructional media center keep pace with the materials and techniques available. It is not enough to build a beautiful building; it is not enough to establish a basic collection of materials; nor is it enough to rest on the traditions and practices handed down from past generations. A media center must continue to provide the best to its faculty and its students. It is a never-ending process. Materials must constantly be previewed, evaluated, and judged to see if they meet the criteria for users. All learning materials should be channeled through the instructional media center, whether they are textbooks, library materials, or professional literature.

The instructional media center must be a center of learning, properly stocked and well organized, staffed with adequate professional and nonprofessional personnel to administer it with one idea in mind, to help students learn. The extent to which the young people of the 1970's will be creative, informed, and knowledgeable is shaped by the content of the materials and the teaching patterns of their instructors.

At Seaside High School, as well as Oak Park and River Forest High School, the best of all possible worlds has been the prime goal —best of facilities, teachers, and materials. A measure of excellence has been realized in these schools. Only the future will record the gains.

CHAPTER 12

A School District IMC

by

KENNETH I. TAYLOR

MANY OF THE EDUCATIONAL CHANGES in Madison that feature non-graded acceleration, conceptual teaching, interdisciplinary instruction, and independent study or creative inquiry would have been difficult to implement without a coordinated instructional media program that extends throughout the school system. Materials programs in Madison schools offer both retrieval and dissemination: retrieval of information, ideas, and concepts originated by others and dissemination by teachers and students of original ideas through media of their own making in accord with their personal styles.

In Madison, IMC and school goals are so closely related that both are planned and discussed as one. Faculty involvement is sought well in advance when an IMC is remodeled, as at Randall Elementary School, or added, as at West Senior High School. When the school is new, early planning is done by the appointed principal, often in consultation with teachers from other schools. A good working relationship is common among central administrators, subject coordinators, buildings and grounds personnel, and the locally appointed architect. Each new media center is seen as a working laboratory whose best features are incorporated into other schools.

Adoption of the IMC Concept

Madison adopted the instructional media center concept in 1964, and implemented the idea in the IMC designs of two new schools, Abraham Lincoln Junior High in 1965 and James Madison Memorial Junior-Senior High in 1966. Both were planned to support modular scheduling, shared teaching, and independent study. In 1965, Madison decentralized audiovisual collections, adding a wider range of media to each school.

Behind this adoption was a history of instructional materials extending back to 1892, when the superintendent requested funds for supplementary books to stimulate student interest in reading. In 1911, the first high school library was established at Central, and in 1925, elementary libraries began at Randall and Emerson.

Today, Madison has 56 schools, 34,000 students, and 1,700 teachers. Each school has an instructional media center with professional and clerical staffs. Centralized ordering and cataloging services, using data processing applications, free staff members from repetitive tasks. On a district basis, Madison averages 13 cataloged items per student, with an annual combined school-year circulation that exceeds one and one-quarter million.

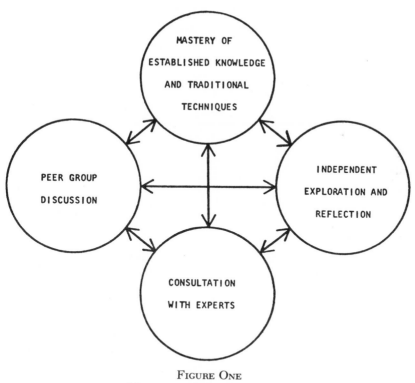

FIGURE ONE
NATURE OF CREATIVE INQUIRY

Creative Inquiry and IMC Design

Theory can be useful in IMC development by explaining why the media program has been established and what the goals are. The Madison theory of creative inquiry has influenced IMC design, facilities, equipment, and staffing.[1]

The first aspect of the theory relates four experiences that are needed for student pursuit of inquiry (Figure One):

1. mastery of established knowledge and traditional techniques;
2. peer group discussion;
3. independent exploration and reflection;
4. consultation with experts.

Each is translated through three design components for group discussion, committee activities, conferences, and independent study.

The second aspect of the theory stresses the need of an original student communication for successful completion of inquiry. This

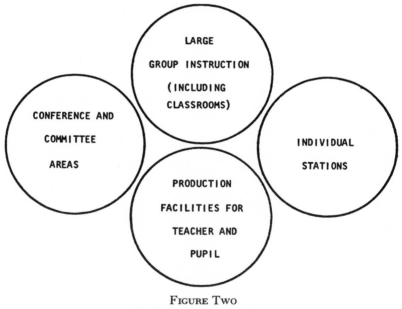

FIGURE TWO
SCHOOL AND IMC FACILITIES FOR CREATIVE INQUIRY

communication synthesizes established knowledge and the student's personal experience. At this point, the student communicates with or through any medium produced by him that is appropriate to his message and his style (Figure Two).

In IMC design, this experience is provided through a fourth design component, production facilities for teacher and pupil. The theory predicts that student production of media may become the fastest growing of all IMC functions.

Educational Functions of the School IMC

IMC design and programs begin with desired educational functions. Some which merit early consideration are as follows:

1. group instruction for common learning;
2. seminars, conferences, and projects involving media;
3. independent inquiry and exploratory examination of materials;
4. production of materials by teachers and pupils for local topics and original communications;
5. reading, listening, and viewing skill development;
6. guidance in the use of school and community resources;
7. preview and selection of curricular related materials;
8. preview and selection of materials appropriate to student interests and maturity levels;
9. preview and selection of materials for faculty in-service growth;
10. in-service programs on media characteristics and use.

If IMCs are planned with instructional programs in mind, what safeguards are available to avoid rigidity in view of inevitable program change? Two answers may be suggested.

First, of the 10 educational functions previously listed, functions one through four are more directly related to design than to media services, requiring translation through special rooms, space allocations, furniture, and equipment. Each anticipates desired methods of teaching and learning. By contrast, the remaining functions follow what the teaching staff chooses to provide. These four functions are accommodated by adequate design and appropriate facilities in sufficient varying degrees, according to the needs of the individual school.

If IMCs are flexible enough to allow proportionate variation in these functions, they will be prepared for program change.

A second answer is that the IMC should be seen as a collective series of evolving, related spaces that are (1) designed for IMC educational functions, (2) located in the IMC core and its counterparts around the building, and (3) equipped to allow teachers and pupils to use and produce materials effectively. These spaces include classroom corner collections, departmental office libraries, laboratory stations, auditoriums, large-group rooms, seminar and conference areas, and subject resource centers. When coordinated and operated as a unit, they are designated as the school IMC complex.

Remodeling in the Elementary School

Unless there is a building addition, the established elementary school often expands its traditional library by adding adjacent classroom

Corridor space was used to widen this IMC and to add production and conference rooms. Emerson Elementary School, Madison Public Schools, Madison, Wisconsin.

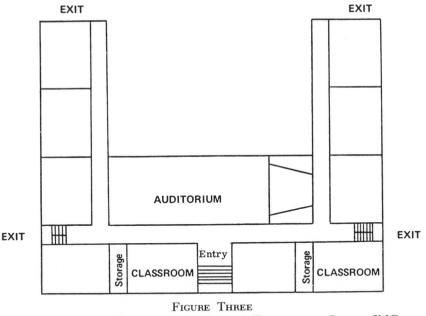

FIGURE THREE
UTILIZATION OF CORRIDORS FOR RANDALL ELEMENTARY SCHOOL IMC
MADISON, WISCONSIN

space. When possible, a long, narrow effect may be avoided by adding corridor space for greater width.

In Madison, two elementary IMCs, Emerson and Randall, have drawn on both classroom and corridor space. Randall also incorporates stairway space. Its former library, added in 1925 but only the size of one classroom, failed to offer the individual and shared media experiences that teachers desired for their pupils. Because the school had five entrances, it was possible to close the major entry and still meet building codes. A floor was built across the double stairwell, classrooms at each side were added, and the corridor was used for greater width. This working area was then adjacent to a level auditorium with a stage, offering potential for a complete, centralized IMC complex (Figure Three).

Corridor space within the new IMC is used for general collections, display, and heavier traffic. The IMC core is designed for independent study, reference, and story telling. Two rooms used for subject collections may be combined, each seating approximately 15 students. Other rooms allow teacher-pupil production and shared listening and viewing. The auditorium, with its original stage, is used for large

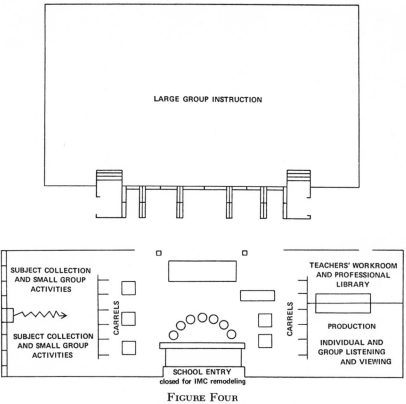

FIGURE FOUR
RANDALL ELEMENTARY SCHOOL IMC
MADISON, WISCONSIN

group instruction, student presentations, and lectures by outside resource persons (Figure Four).

Two years prior to remodeling, Randall teachers began a study of
the IMC concept, moving from theory to functions, program, and
media selection. Their educational specifications provided a foundation for design that reflected their instructional program. The IMC is
informal in operation, with students using a great variety of media
alone and together. Projects are developed by students in consultation with their teachers and the IMC staff. Many of the media created by students have been added to the school collection for others
to use.

Although remodeling involves problems not encountered in new
buildings, it may offer unusual opportunities to capture the beauty of
old architectural features. By creating stark white arches at corridor

The established school may offer unusual opportunities for capturing the beauty of old architectural features through remodeling. Randall Elementary School IMC, Madison, Wisconsin.

openings, introducing open beams under high ceilings, adding walnut paneling, and bringing in red brick of the original school walls, Architects Bowen and Kamazawa created in this sixty-year-old building one of the most beautiful elementary IMCs in Madison.

Elementary Schools and Nongraded Programs

In a new building, the IMC and related teaching-learning spaces must be located for maximum correlation of materials and instructional programs. Classrooms should be clustered for shared teaching, modifications in group size, and accessibility to IMC resources.

At John Muir Elementary School (1968), the building was designed for nongraded acceleration (Figure Five). Its predecessor, Huegel Elementary School (1966), is a round building with an IMC circled by classrooms. John Muir achieves equal flexibility within a rectangular building. Classrooms, grouped in triads, may be combined. Each room has a separate entry into the IMC. At the entrances, natural pods may be used for small-group tasks. The IMC core is open and flexible, with movable shelving, furniture, and equipment located to

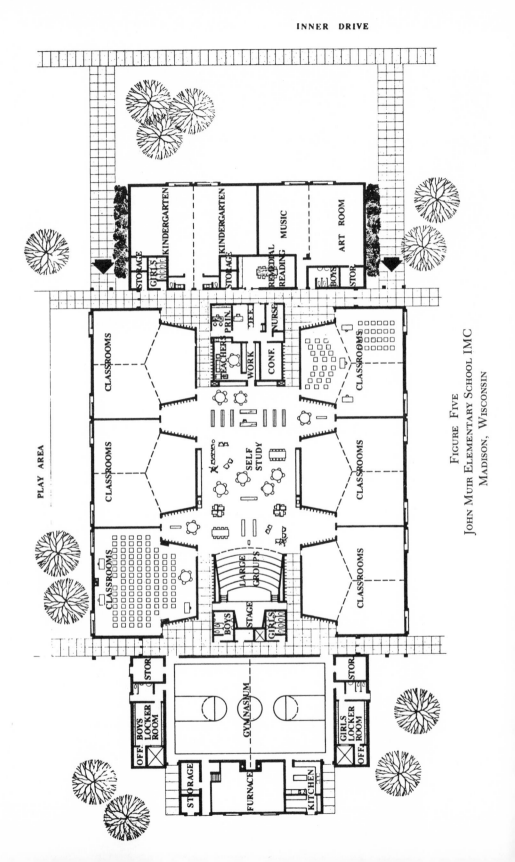

FIGURE FIVE
JOHN MUIR ELEMENTARY SCHOOL IMC
MADISON, WISCONSIN

Designed as a series of giant, carpeted steps, this large-group instruction room may become an extension of the IMC core. View from the stage, John Muir Elementary School, Madison, Wisconsin.

define study areas and traffic patterns. Counters and carrels are available for individual reading, listening, and viewing. At one end, a large-group instruction room, designed as a series of giant, carpeted steps without chairs or desks, may be opened as an extension of the IMC core.

Whenever specialized equipment, such as a dry mount press or thermocopier, is needed, students create their material in the IMC core and pods or in art and classrooms. Student production of materials is one of degree, with newer equipment and techniques introduced as they appear.

General Instructional, Administrative, and Organizational Characteristics of Madison IMCs

Program operation makes materials available to students with a minimum of difficulty and assists students in their use. Below are specifications in Madison school IMC handbooks which apply to all schools.

— Skill development and guidance in materials use is shared by IMC staff members and teachers in the IMC and in classrooms.

— Faculty in-service programs on media use are planned by IMC staff members and teachers.

— All materials are available to students and teachers for use in the IMC, around the school, and at home.

— Students have access to the IMC before, after, and during any part of the school day.

— Students are encouraged to draw upon all resources as needed for classroom related activities.

— Students are encouraged to engage at will in leisurely, individual, and even aimless examination of materials for personal exploration and discovery.

— Materials are purchased on recommendations of and in consultation with pupils and teachers.

— Materials are obtained on loan from outside resources.

— Materials are produced by students, teachers, and IMC staff members to meet local school needs.

— IMCs are used by individuals, by small groups, by classes attending with their teachers, by classes under the direction and guidance of IMC members, and by more than one class participating in large group instruction.

— Student and teacher use of materials is flexible and free.

— Traffic flow in and out of the IMC occurs at any time.

— Attendance loads rise to maximum highs and fall to relative lows during the day, depending upon instructional and learning requirements.

— Collections are located to encourage exploration among books, filmstrips, records and other media.

— Central records indicate locations of materials in the IMC and on extended loan throughout the school.

— Professional collections are located in the IMC, in teacher workrooms, or in any other convenient part of the school.

— Simply operated viewing, listening, and production equipment is accessible to students and ready for use with a minimum of difficulty.

— IMCs are planned and equipped for a maximum degree of flexibility.

— Facilities are designed for group instruction, conferences and projects, and independent study.

— Independent study stations are located away from heavy traffic areas to insure a minimum of distractions.

— Reference collections of frequently consulted media are located near the entry of the IMC.

— Specialized instructional and learning areas in the IMC and around the building are designed to accommodate effective and efficient use of media and equipment.

— Specialized IMC instructional areas are planned in number and purpose with reference to similar areas around the building.

Distinctive Characteristics of Elementary School IMCs

— The IMC is informal in atmosphere and operation.

— The IMC is attractive, inviting, and designed to create pride in one's school.

— Because their interests are often spontaneous and short-lived, students are encouraged to use the IMC at any time.

— Students use all media and related equipment independently and in groups.

— A major part of a student's time in the IMC is spent on small group projects.

— Independent study projects are of relatively short duration.

— Students create simple materials of their own.

— Inviting, casual storytelling facilities are a dominant feature.

— Weekly scheduling of upper grades is deemphasized in favor of class visits as required for classroom related activities.

— Group instruction is informal, lively, often spontaneous, with a high degree of student response and participation.

The Junior High or Middle School

Although it is called a junior high school, La Follette serves as a middle school laboratory for grades six through eight. If successful, its program may be extended to other Madison junior highs. Opened during the 1968–69 school year, La Follette was designed to provide

flexible facilities for conceptual teaching, which emphasizes interdisciplinary relationships and individualized instruction.

Planning for the school proceeded along four lines:

1. building design that modifies traditional departmental isolation;
2. administrative principles related to teaching assignments, class
size, and student schedules;
3. curriculum models that highlight interdisciplinary concepts but
allow freedom in implementation;
4. in-service training for teachers covering learning theory, adoles-
cent development, anthropology, conceptual teaching, and individualized instruction.

Because the middle school should provide a transitional program
that is distinctive for students at this age, its curriculum and instruction depart from the preparatory school emphasis of the traditional
junior high. The first curriculum models for La Follette were developed in the summer of 1968 by teachers from several of Madison's
schools, providing common experiences in science, social studies, and
language arts.

Within the seventh grade key or year-length concept, "Man Meets
His Needs in Various Ways," model one focuses on the subconcept,
"This is a beautiful earth, but some of its resources are irreplaceable."
Beginning with Madison water pollution problems, the model uses a
community topic to make the student aware of a need for learning
through a number of current resources. Instructional strategy begins
with a multimedia presentation by the teacher on water use in the
city, raising questions that are of immediate concern to Madison. A
second phase draws upon geographic and scientific materials for information, using literary materials to dramatize values and ambiva-
lent attitudes of man toward his physical environment. Students are
involved through cooperative activities that include a newspaper on
Madison and role playing which simulates a Common Council meeting. Individual study branches from the central topic by focusing on
other physical resources.

Curriculum models for each grade provide understandings, behavioral goals, media, learning experiences, and evaluation in outline
form, allowing teacher freedom in implementation. Recommended
media include textbook, library, and audiovisual materials. Learning
experiences make great use of community resources. New curriculum

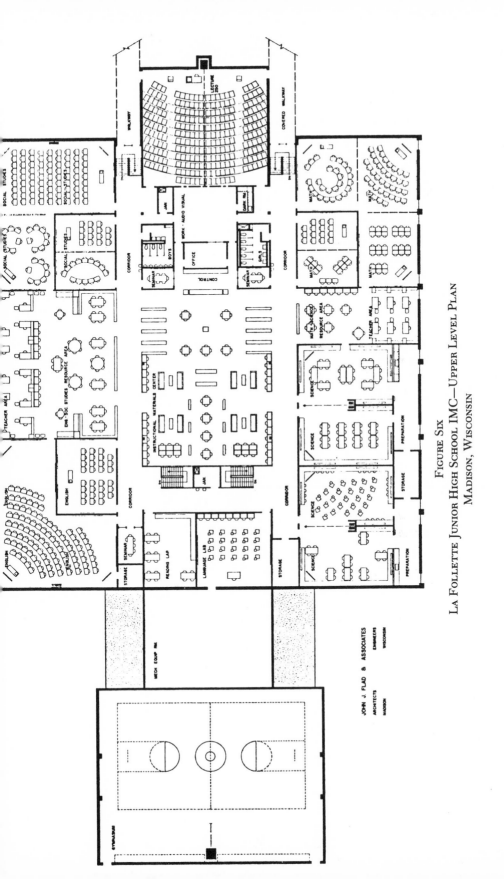

FIGURE SIX
LA FOLLETTE JUNIOR HIGH SCHOOL IMC—UPPER LEVEL PLAN
MADISON, WISCONSIN

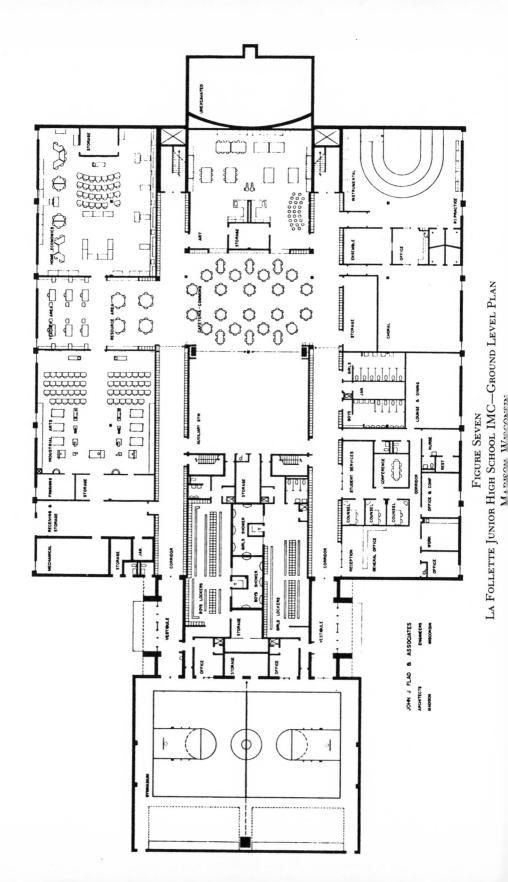

FIGURE SEVEN
LA FOLLETTE JUNIOR HIGH SCHOOL IMC—GROUND LEVEL PLAN
MADISON, WISCONSIN

JOHN J FLAD & ASSOCIATES
ARCHITECTS
MADISON
ENGINEERS
WISCONSIN

models and teaching methods for La Follette may take three or more years to develop. In addition to commercial materials, La Follette must also produce its own, many of an audiovisual nature, for teachers and students. At many points, students must also create materials to express their solutions to local problems.

The IMC core is located on the second level of the school (Figure Six), with spaces defined by movable equipment. Seminar rooms and production facilities are in proximity, with an adjacent large-group instruction room that is designed for formal use of audiovisual materials. Reading and language laboratories are nearby. At either side, interdisciplinary resource centers offer special collections, with space for teacher-pupil consultation. In Madison, these are the first subject resource centers designed for a junior high. On the ground level, a resource center is shared by industrial arts and home economics (Figure Seven).

Because of its interest to other Madison schools, this program is a joint responsibility of the individual school and the district. An in-service program uses locally produced materials on new teaching methods which have been prepared for possible later use in other schools.

Distinctive Characteristics
of Junior High or Middle School IMCs

— The IMC is both formal and informal in atmosphere and operation.

— The IMC offers transitional experiences leading from group orientation of the elementary school to self-directed pursuits required by the senior high.

— Students divide their time between group projects and independent study.

— More emphasis than in elementary schools is placed on reserved materials, note-taking, and systematic organization of materials over a greater period of time.

— Independent study projects are of short or relatively long duration, depending upon student ability and maturity.

— Students create more advanced instructional materials for themselves, including audio tapes, photographs, slides, and transparencies.

— Standard and electronic equipment, such as microfilm readers and remote access to audio tapes, is introduced to develop research skills needed for senior high.

— Group instruction takes on formal aspects.

Independent Study in the Senior High School

To augment independent study on the scale now being tried in many of the nation's senior high schools, a school must give early consideration to a full complement of media services and collections that extend throughout the building. James Madison Memorial Senior High illustrates the early evolution of the IMC core and related spaces for an instructional program that required greater access to materials than is possible on a completely centralized basis. Opening in 1966, the school maintained a traditional program for one year while the faculty planned administrative and instructional procedures for modular scheduling, shared teaching, pupil-teacher conferences, and independent study.

IMC facilities available on opening day are illustrated in Figure Eight. Its proportion of independent stations was greater than in any other Madison school. Carrels in the middle offer dial access to an automatic audiotape deck. Those at the outside are unwired. Other areas of the IMC are formally defined for individual and group use and production of media. The large-group instruction room, which may be divided, offers rear screen projection for multimedia presentations.

Although these facilities provided an excellent complement of centralized media services and collections, the school's plan for independent study required additional collections and study spaces. For the second year, four subject resource centers were opened, operating in conjunction with the IMC core.

Media in these subject resource centers are more specialized than in the IMC core, including multiple copies of pamphlets, models, multimedia kits, and supplementary texts, in addition to traditional printed and audiovisual materials. Resource specialists, one for each center, have generally had at least a bachelor's degree, but no library science or audiovisual training. All work under the direction of the professional IMC staff. Although each subject resource center has a catalog of its holdings, its collections also are recorded in the main catalog of the IMC core. Media also are placed on extended loan in other instructional areas of the school.

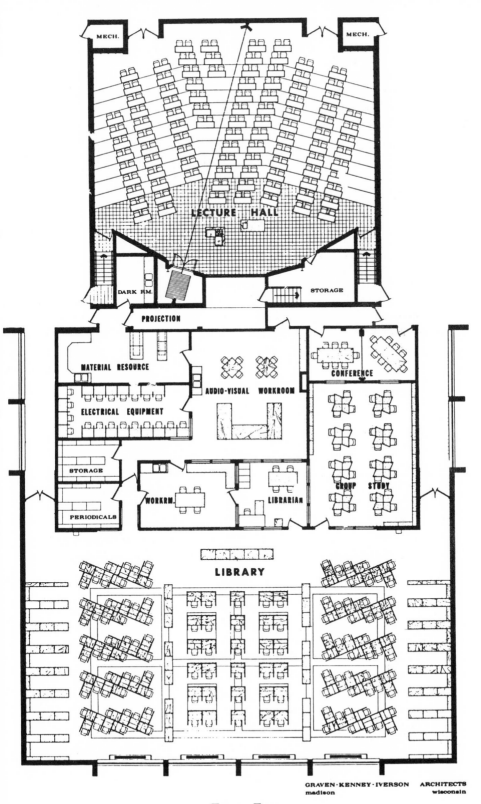

MECH.   MECH.

LECTURE HALL

DARK RM.   STORAGE

PROJECTION

MATERIAL RESOURCE   CONFERENCE

AUDIO-VISUAL   WORKROOM

ELECTRICAL EQUIPMENT

STORAGE   GROUP STUDY

WORKRM.   LIBRARIAN

PERIODICALS

LIBRARY

GRAVEN·KENNEY·IVERSON   ARCHITECTS
madison   wisconsin

FIGURE EIGHT
JAMES MADISON MEMORIAL HIGH SCHOOL IMC, MADISON, WISCONSIN

The subject resource center offers specialized collections in convenient locations around the school. James Madison Memorial High School, Madison, Wisconsin.

It is already evident that these subject resource centers have helped students find specialized media in convenient locations. Guidance is available from either subject resource specialists or teachers. While it is probable that four centers represent too high a degree of diversification, available facilities and the time factor at James Madison made this number feasible. Additional time is needed for the James Madison media and instructional programs to mature. Nevertheless, subject resource center support has been convincing enough to have been adopted in modified form at La Follette Junior High School.

Distinctive Characteristics of Senior High IMCs

— The IMC is more formal in atmosphere and operation than junior highs but flow of activities is free and easy.

— Emphasis is on student independence and self-reliance in locating information and appropriate materials.

— Independent projects are frequently of long duration.

— Students combine independent study, small-group discussion, and teacher conferences in order to plan, pursue, and complete complex individual projects.

— Great use is made of outside resources.

— Specialized collections and related study areas are developed around the building to supplement the more general resources of the main IMC.

— Electronic equipment, such as dial access to audio- and video-tapes, is introduced to assure efficient use of reserved media.

—Students create advanced materials of their own, such as video-tapes, individually and in groups.

— Specialized instructional areas are developed as needed around the building.

Staffing the IMC

IMC programs require specialized tasks of professional and supportive personnel. Staff positions now found in Madison's school IMCs include library and audiovisual consultants and a laboratory teacher, all professionals; a clerical library aide and a clerk-typist; an intern, who is a library school student; and a subject resource center specialist.

There are library consultants and library aide/clerk-typists in every school. Audiovisual consultants are on the staff in every senior high and are being added to junior high IMCs. They work with library consultants as a team. Only Shorewood Elementary has a laboratory teacher in an experimental IMC laboratory designed for independent projects. College interns from library schools are placed in IMCs as available. Two or three are employed full time on a one-semester basis. The subject resource specialist must have a minimum of two years of college, but he almost always has at least a bachelor's degree.

In any IMC with more than one professional person, one is designated as head in elementary and junior high and as chairman in senior high, with responsibility for coordinating the program.

The Audiovisual Consultant

The professional audiovisual consultant position, as defined in Madison, has been of special interest to other schools. Madison's emphasis upon student production of media requires an audiovisual consultant with specialized training that complements the skills of the library consultant. The audiovisual consultant is a co-worker with library consultants, all of whom work with students as well as teachers.

The audiovisual consultant establishes stations for listening and viewing. He assists students in their search for audiovisual media, develops their skills in evaluating media, and trains them in production methods. He selects appropriate audiovisual media for the school in consultation with the IMC staff and all school personnel, doing so with reference to what is available in printed collections. Today, Madison has audiovisual consultants in every senior high and in one-third of its junior highs, adding them as available and as programs require their services.

Working together, library and audiovisual consultants gain on the job a more comprehensive understanding of the entire range of media than they receive in college. A case study of audiovisual–library professional relationships within the IMC has been presented in a multimedia curriculum package, produced by the IMC staff at Gompers Junior High School.[2]

Given below is the Madison position description for audiovisual consultant.

AUDIOVISUAL CONSULTANT

General Characteristics

Recruited by:	Director of Personnel.
Elected by:	Board of Education.
Term of Election:	One year.

Working Relationships

Reports to:	Head, Instructional Media Center.
Receives Guidance from:	Coordinator of Audiovisual Materials. Coordinator of Library Services. School Principal and Teachers.
Extent of Guidance Received:	Information and recommendations pertaining to service, selection of materials, and guidance in the use of materials needed for the development of an instructional media center and program.
Supervises:	No one.

Provides Guidance to: School Principal, Teachers, and
                                         Pupils.

Special Characteristics of the Position

Required Experience or   Required audiovisual and teach-
   Training: ing credentials of Wisconsin; ap-
                                         preciation of the concept of an
                                         instructional media center.

Desired Experience or Training: Master's degree in audiovisual
                                         education or instructional media;
                                         experience in a school instruc-
                                         tional media center; introductory
                                         training in library science and
                                         administration of school library
                                         services.

Special Requirements of the   Broad understanding of the in-
   Position: structional media center and pro-
                                         gram; ability to relate instruc-
                                         tional materials and appropriate
                                         technological equipment and
                                         their use to the school educa-
                                         tional program.

Principal Characteristics of Work

Types of Activities Performed   Works with teachers and pupils
   Frequently: to promote effective use of au-
                                         diovisual materials and equip-
                                         ment, and, when relevant,
                                         printed materials; seeks to en-
                                         courage multimedia use of mate-
                                         rials for teaching and learning
                                         purposes; assists in the develop-
                                         ment of in-service programs or
                                         media.

Types of Activities Performed   Participates in local professional
   Occasionally: media activities.

Basic Function

Promotes school-wide use of audiovisual materials and equipment with
reference to printed materials and contributes to the development of
the school instructional media center program.

Position Responsibilities

I. Program Development
   Supports and maintains a coordinated program of printed and audiovisual materials and services for all school personnel.

Views the instructional media center as a laboratory for research and study where pupils learn to work alone and in groups under the direction of the media center staff and their teachers.

Recognizes the instructional media center as an evolving and expanding services and communications agency which exists to support the school curriculum and educational objectives of students and teachers.

Encourages student and teacher use of printed and audiovisual materials in a multimedia approach toward learning and instruction.

II. Faculty Services

Works closely with teachers to make the instructional media center of optimum service to them.

Evaluates and selects audiovisual, and when appropriate, related printed materials in personal consultation with teachers.

Prepares bibliographies of audiovisual materials for teachers. With other instructional media center staff members adds appropriate related printed materials.

With other instructional media center staff members, assists in planning and participates in workshops and in-service programs designed to promote effective use of materials and services by teachers.

Acquaints teachers and library consultants with newer technological developments in the audiovisual field and works with them to determine potential contributions to teaching methods.

Makes audiovisual and other materials easily accessible to teachers.

Trains teachers and library consultants in basic methods of production and works with them to determine when local production of materials is advantageous.

With the assistance of the Coordinator of Audiovisual Services, acts as faculty advisor on the selection and purchase of new audiovisual equipment.

Establishes effective organizational and technical routines for the use and maintenance of building audiovisual equipment.

Assists teachers in development of classroom and large group multimedia presentations.

III. Pupil Guidance

Works closely with pupils to insure their success in independent and group research activities.

Teaches students how to use audiovisual and related printed materials intelligently and effectively.

Uses, when appropriate, innovative procedures such as large group instruction, to teach student use of instructional media most effectively.

Encourages elementary production of materials by pupils to capitalize on the advantages of visual presentation for individual and group reports. Makes elementary production facilities and equipment available to pupils.

Assists in the training and continuing education of student assistants, seeking, in cooperation with library consultants, to acquaint them with a broad range of media and related services.

Acquaints student assistants and other pupils with opportunities in the field of audiovisual education as a profession.

IV. Selection of Materials

Evaluates and selects audiovisual materials with reference to what is already available in the school collection of printed materials.

Selects materials in consultation with teachers and with reference to curricular needs.

Makes recommendations for the evaluation and selection of printed materials to the library consultants.

Has knowledge of and uses the most frequently consulted selection tools for printed materials.

Draws upon outside media and service agencies when necessary to take full advantage of the resources of the Madison community.

Assists in developing audiovisual and related collections that reflect the broad range of pupil interest and that meet their different levels of maturity and ability.

V. Staff Relationships

Assists the head of the instructional media center in developing and maintaining a coordinated program of instructional media and services.

Plans with other audiovisual and library consultants effective methods of promoting pupil and teacher use of the instructional media center.

Seeks the assistance of library consultants in developing a growing knowledge of library materials, equipment, and services.

Advises other instructional media center staff members on selection and use of audiovisual equipment to be used by students and teachers in the instructional media center.

IMC Equipment for Student Use

To offer opportunities for student listening, viewing, and production of materials, the IMC must have equipment that is available to students in sufficient quantity at any time. It must be simple to operate and ready to use.

Although state and national guidelines give standards for audiovisual equipment to be used by teachers, few if any are concerned with equipment for student use in the school IMC. Given below in abridged form are the 1969 Madison standards for equipment to be used by students. They offer a minimum foundation for each school and assure balance in district budgeting.

Audiovisual Equipment	Elementary	Junior	Senior
Map print cabinet (for art prints, maps, and poster board)	One	One	One
Phonograph	Minimum of 3, plus 1 for every 250 students or major portion thereof over 500	Minimum of 3, plus 1 for every 250 students or major portion thereof over 500	Minimum of 4, plus 1 for every 400 students or major portion thereof over 1,200
Tape recorder	Minimum of 2, plus 1 for every 250 students or major portion thereof over 500	Minimum of 2, plus 1 for every 250 students or major portion thereof over 500	Minimum of 3, plus 1 for every 400 students or major portion thereof over 1,200
Headphones	Minimum of 10, plus 2 for every 250 students or major portion thereof over 500	Minimum of 10, plus 2 for every 250 students or major portion thereof over 500	Minimum of 2 for every phonograph and tape recorder
Easel for art print display	One (optional)	One (optional)	One (optional)
Filmstrip previewer	Minimum of 5, plus 1 for every 250 students or major portion thereof over 500	Minimum of 5, plus 1 for every 250 students or major portion thereof over 500	Minimum of 4, plus 1 for every 250 students or major portion thereof over 500
Overhead projector	One	One	One
Dry mount press	One	One	One
Thermocopy	One (optional)	One	One
Primary typewriter, 6 pitch (for production)	One in IMC or school	One	One
Microfilm reader	None	One (optional)	One for every 300 students

Audiovisual Equipment	Elementary	Junior	Senior
Microfilm reader-printer	None	None	One
AM-FM Radio	One	One	One
Phonograph record browser bin (100 records)	One	One	One
Phonograph record browser unit, free standing (250 records)	One	One	One
Copy stand and camera for slides and prints	One (optional)	One (optional)	One (optional)
35mm camera	One (optional)	One (optional)	One (optional)
8mm motion picture camera and projector	One (optional)	One (optional)	One (optional)
TV receivers	One	As needed	As needed
8mm single-concept projector, with stop feature	One standard & one super 8	One standard & one super 8	One standard & one super 8

Many Madison school IMCs are well above the stated minimums in this annually revised list. A similar Madison guide is available for equipment to be used by teachers.

Plans for the Future

Although IMCs have their roots in libraries and classrooms of the past, their growth has been most dramatic within the past decade. Today the IMC is accepted as a vital part of any contemporary instructional program, traditional or experimental. The major question facing schools is how to realize IMC potential through the best instructional strategies available.

Instructional and media programs become one as schools use materials within broader experiences that originate and remain under the direction of the teacher. Valuable time is lost whenever it is proposed that media—the text, the motion picture, the programmed book, or television broadcast—can teach by themselves; for each time this is attempted, the results are disappointing. Today's materials are still designed to be inserted at proper times into larger frames of reference.

What of the IMC of the future? Madison believes that it soon may become an instructional agency in its own right, with communication as its proper subject matter, embracing man's efforts to communicate with others through symbols unique to the sciences, social sciences, and appreciative arts. Within IMC collections are numerous records in printed, pictorial, and audio form containing these symbols. The IMC may become the best agency in the school for teaching students how to interpret the symbols of others, and, in turn, to use similar symbols for original communications to their colleagues, with or entirely through media.

PART IV

THE SUMMARY

CHAPTER 13

The IMC: Future Prospects

by

MARVIN GRANDSTAFF

An associate professor in the College of Education, Michigan State University, Marvin Grandstaff is experienced in the field of instructional media. He developed and supervised an experimental program in curriculum design on the secondary level in a Kansas high school and helped devise a curriculum for the gifted in Illinois.

The recipient of an Ed.D. from Indiana University, Dr. Grandstaff has taught at Indiana University and the University of Texas at El Paso. He is the co-editor, with Cole Brembeck of Michigan State, of Readings in the Social Foundations of Education. *He has also written a number of articles, including "Secrecy, Sanity and the Schools" and "Power, Freedom and Educational Revolution," both published in* School and Society.

EDUCATIONAL PROGRESS may come from many sources: from the impact of a leader's personality; through the careful and convincing demonstration of a new device or method; or, in an almost revolutionary manner, through the demands of a large group of people who wish to see an existing practice changed. In less dramatic cases, the impetus to progress may be no more than a popularization of a name clarifying and extending an idea that has long been known. This last mode, which indicates a substantial change, not merely a nominal change, characterizes the recent emphasis given to the instructional media center. The concept has existed a long time—since libraries first became centers for study and learning and ceased to be simple depositories for manuscripts. The magnificent library of Alexander the Great provides a historically remote instance of the concept of the instructional media center in operation.

The tremendous output of materials—books, films, filmstrips, tapes, programmed learning devices, and so on—during the last few years has heightened interest in the entire field of instructional materials. The new emphasis upon excellence and rigor in public education has served to point out the sad inadequacy of many of our present materials and the need, not only for better and more systematically structured materials, but also for better ways of manipulating and processing new materials. With these needs in mind educators examined past practices, found one that was capable of dealing with the problem at hand, and put a new name to it. The result was the instructional media center. The tasks that remain are to clarify this concept and to provide a modern image that will replace its time-honored antecedent—the library.

There are many strategic and political factors involved in proposing and implementing educational change, especially if the change is radical. Educators, parents, and even children do not always react to innovation with unbridled delight, an innovation may upset the comfortable status quo. Frequently a proposal for radical change must be compromised, modified, and mutilated beyond recognition in order to be put into practice. Answers must be ready for such questions as "But doesn't that take the teacher out of teaching?" or "What will it cost?" or "How will you ever get parents to accept it?"

Educators who undertake educational reform should have a vision of what they might hope to achieve so they do not become too easily satisfied with less. Such problems of conceptualization are prior to, and distinct from, the problems of implementing an instructional media center. Therefore, the concept of the IMC will be clarified; then some potential areas of conceptual difficulty will be pointed out.

The Concept of an Instructional Media Center

Very simply, this writer believes that the IMC may be defined as a systematic structuring of materials, equipment, and services available to students and teachers for utilization in learning. The fact that teachers will use many of the materials for teaching is incidental because the ultimate outcome is still learning. Therefore the IMC is defined primarily in terms of its function. The center is a place for students and teachers, either independently or cooperatively, to engage in learning activities as widely varied as discussions, reading, listening to recordings, writing, viewing and producing materials for classroom use. The concept of the IMC also includes the organizational arrangements applied to the materials, equipment, and services in order to fulfill the function. These may be classified into four tasks: the collection, categorization, evaluation, and distribution of materials and equipment, as well as services.

When the scope of collected knowledge was very limited and when the means for making permanent records of knowledge were restricted, the tasks involved were fairly simple. Socrates was, in a real sense, his own instructional media center. As knowledge became more voluminous and the records of knowledge became easier to produce, institutions arose for the specific purpose of storing accumulated knowledge-bearing documents. Libraries have customarily done a good job of the first task, the collection of materials. If there is a unique educational imperative to which the concept of the IMC is applicable, it is to do much more in the areas of categorization, evaluation, and distribution than has been done in the past. In these areas many conceptual difficulties arise.

Notions of categorization must be reexamined to seek new and more educationally fruitful conceptual structures into which to cast this staggering collection. The full function of the IMC requires the use of its collected information by learners, and the degree to which it can be used depends largely upon the efficiency of the categories.

Procedures for evaluating materials also need to be reexamined. Educators have labored too long with grossly inadequate materials. They have taught with biased, outdated, or erroneous materials because nothing else was available. But today, as schools increase the stock of available materials, diversification is possible. At least part of the blame for the problem of inadequate materials is the absence of effective decision-making procedures and evaluative techniques. Obviously, some materials are more educationally efficacious than others. To leave the evaluation of the educational worth of materials to chance or to the whims of commercial publishers is an unsound policy.

Among the four tasks, present practices are perhaps most remiss in the area of distribution. Media other than books have not been available in conventional libraries. In contrast, the IMC has been specifically designed to effect improvements in distribution.

With the four tasks of the IMC in mind, let us now consider the long-range possibilities and potentialities of the IMC concept.

The Technological Revolution

Many contemporary commentators see the current technological revolution as comparable to the Industrial Revolution. Machines are now replacing not just physical labor, but tedious and repetitious mental tasks. One reaction to this computer revolution is fear and horror. At first glance, man appears destined to become obsolete—a slave to, if not entirely superseded by, his marvelous thinking machines. This reaction is especially widespread among teachers. Any proposal to technologize education is viewed with alarm and indignation, purportedly because a necessary condition of learning is personal involvement between two people—the teacher and the learner. However, there is no adequate warrant for the assumption that learning must entail a teacher. If the full potential of the IMC concept is to be realized, the assumption of "teacher" as a necessary concomitant of "learner" must be seriously reconsidered.

In *The Liberal Hour*, Kenneth Galbraith [1] takes an optimistic view of the computer revolution. He points out the great human potential that can accrue when the human mind is liberated from tasks that are fundamentally mundane, and he argues convincingly that the emerging computer technology actually frees man for those activities that are uniquely human. In this view, the new technology is not a threat but a blessing; it does not devalue man but rather elevates him to a significant place in the scheme of the universe. This more optimistic interpretation has much to offer education and is particularly relevant to the concept of the IMC.

Suppose the IMC could incorporate many of the time-consuming but basically mechanical tasks that teachers now perform. Suppose that whenever learners desire information they could go not to a teacher or to a traditional library but to a highly technological IMC. What would such a situation look like? Picture first the physical features of this Utopian learning environment and then the activities and functions of some of its human components.

The Learning Center of the Future

The sheer amount of accumulated information is staggering, and any of that information may be relevant and important to a learning activity being carried on by a student. Just the storage of information, especially in its traditional forms, creates a problem in physical facilities. The use of microfilms and of computers as information storage devices has begun to deal with this problem. Certainly, given the limitations of present computer technology, every learning center cannot expect to possess a relatively complete information storage facility, but just as certainly the hypothetical situation must include a facility for storing a substantial body of information. Thus, the first physical feature of the learning center of the future is a central computer system to store large quantities of information. In addition, it may be possible to link these storage facilities with other similar facilities.

A much-publicized exhibit at a meeting in St. Louis of the American Library Association was a small computer that was linked by telephone to a much larger computer in New York. One could request material on a wide range of topics, and the small computer forwarded the inquiry by telephone to New York. Within a matter of minutes the machine in St. Louis printed out the computer in New York. It is not too difficult to imagine a nation-wide network of information storage facilities linked electronically, with devices to tie into the network incorporated into school facilities.

Storage facilities need not be limited to items of information. It is technically quite easy to store large quantities of printed material on microfilm and to make the retrieval of such materials a quick and mechanical operation. Microfilming, along with the promise of increasingly efficient and economical means of reproduction of materials, greatly minimizes the problem posed by the need for multiple copies of printed and plane-surface visual materials.

Thus, the learning center of the future features a multifunctional facility of considerable size, consisting of a central computerized storage center and the required auxiliary storage devices. Supplementing these would be adequate facilities for use: study booths with equipment for performing simple information retrieval operations, microfilm viewing screens, listening devices for taped materials, machines for administering programmed materials, tape recorders, typewriters, and so on; small- and large-group class meeting rooms with electronic access to stored information; central catalogs of available material, electronically coded, compact and easy to operate; and planning centers for teachers and technology specialists.

Educational Personnel and Educational Technology

Information storage is only a starting point. Obviously, it is possible to store huge quantities of information that will never be used. Information retrieval could be as difficult as getting a book out of a library. At this point the human components of the system become crucial. Given a large amount of stored information, small quantities may be taken out in an almost unrestricted number of ways. The problem of which combination to utilize is a human one. Machines will never be any better than the questions men are able to frame for them. A computer is neutral; it will as readily retrieve information about the price of eggs in China as on the philosophy of Plato.

If maximum use is to be made of the rich potentials of technology, educators especially must realize that the human component must be capable of exploiting that potential; the men and women who work with these machines must be specialists. The computers cannot work effectively for education unless educational specialists in computer technology are available and adequately prepared to operate them. On a smaller scale, one wonders how much equipment for teaching developmental reading—tachistoscopes, reading pacers, and so on— is idle in the schools because teachers lack the mechanical skills necessary to put them to use; how many NDEA-purchased bioscopes are gathering dust on laboratory shelves because no one knows how to use them; or, on an even more mundane level, how many films are not shown simply because teachers do not want to bother threading the projector.

Obviously, the idea of the educational technologist is also relevant in other areas. Using the complex and diverse equipment in today's IMC demands a high degree of skill and competence, skill that is not acquired by taking a one-semester audiovisual course or by watching a salesman's demonstration. If even the present automated devices are to be used effectively, personnel must be encouraged to specialize in the emerging technology of instruction. Such specialists in the methods of handling materials would have a very important and sophisticated job. On these educational technologists would fall most of the responsibility for the invention of novel and educationally fruitful ways of programming materials.

Another area calling for specialization is the field of evaluation. Only a specialist in the content and utility analysis of materials could perform this function; the scope of materials is so wide that it would be unreasonable to expect one teacher to evaluate them all. The available specialists in this area, instruction and curriculum directors, are rather few and burdened with administrative duties. Unfortunately, the necessary specialized training is not conventionally offered at the undergraduate level; in fact, special training in material content is seldom accessible below the doctoral level. At present, teachers are trained for conventional educational programs, and specialization comes later, if at all. There seems little reason why specialization could not begin much sooner. The problems are complex, but present patterns make specialization desirable; potential developments make it crucial.

The Designer of Learning Experiences

No matter how complete and well-staffed this highly technological learning center may be, the distribution function will depend largely upon the quality and direction of learning. Given efficient learning devices, there must be an agency to mediate between the learner and the devices, and that agency is obviously the teacher. The idea of mediating, of directing learning, gives a new dimension to the conventional role of the teacher. Hypothesize a few situations in order to see how the designer of learning—the teacher—fits into the scheme.

Suppose a teacher is a specialist in reading instruction. His task might become that of diagnosing reading skills and patterns and making suggestions for program designs for individual students. With the cooperation of evaluation and cataloging specialists, he could set up the facilities of the learning center for individual learners or for small groups of learners and then work directly with the students to evaluate the outcomes of the carefully designed learning programs. Or a social studies director might develop a series of learning exercises for a student seminar group. In conjunction with other specialists, he would draw up a list of materials and have the appropriate retrieval program made up, so that the students might have easy access to the necessary materials. Finally, a designer of learning might work with a student on an individual study project. He would not function as the fountainhead of truth, but rather assist the student in formulating the right questions to take to the learning center.

Not all educational personnel are capable of directing learning in this way, but if the IMC concept were fully developed, there would be many other avenues for educational contribution. In addition, those who have the capability for guiding learning would not need to be burdened with other important, but fundamentally different, responsibilities.

The Unforeseeables

Some of the most significant prospects and problems of the IMC concept have been sketched. Certainly there are many practical difficulties: a really complete IMC may be very costly, and its effective use could make tremendous demands upon educational personnel and upon present patterns and conceptions of staffing. The kind of learning environment projected here is not a blueprint for an IMC of the future. It is only a partial projection. Change is certain enough that educators can expect new prospects and new problems. The point is simply that today's planners cannot afford to be easily satisfied with today's progress. They must make projections with vision so that today's blueprint will not be obsolete tomorrow.

CHAPTER 14

The IMC: A Selected, Annotated Bibliography

by

HAROLD S. DAVIS

BOOKS AND PAMPHLETS

American Association of School Librarians and the Department of Audiovisual Instruction. *Standards for School Media Programs.* Chicago: American Library Association; and Washington, D.C.: National Education Association, 1969. 66 pages.

The new standards developed by the AASL and DAVI.

Beggs, David W., III. *Decatur-Lakeview High School: A Practical Application of the Trump Plan.* Englewood Cliffs, N.J.: Prentice-Hall, 1964. 260 pages.

The characteristics and uses of the IMC are discussed on pages 142–49.

Benyon, John. *Study Carrels: Designs for Independent Study Space.* Stanford, Calif.: Western Regional Center of Educational Facilities Laboratories, Stanford University, 1964. 20 pages.

A booklet showing carrels of all types from the simple to the sophisticated.

Brown, James W., and James W. Thornton, Jr., eds. *New Media in Higher Education.* Washington, D.C.: National Education Association, 1963. 182 pages.

Although most of the book is devoted to uses of new media, Chapter V describes several college IMCs.

Dale, Edgar. *Audiovisual Methods in Teaching.* 3rd ed. New York: Holt, Rinehart and Winston, 1969. 719 pages.

The book contains three parts: (1) theory and practice of audiovisual teaching, (2) media and materials of audiovisual teaching, and (3) systems and technology in teaching. The final chapter describes how to organize and coordinate the use of instructional materials.

Davis, Harold S. *How to Organize an Effective Team Teaching Program.* Englewood Cliffs, N.J.: Prentice-Hall, 1966. 64 pages.
Pages 53–56 describe the advantages of study in an instructional materials center.

De Bernardis, Amo. *Planning Schools for New Media.* Portland, Ore.: Portland Public Schools and the Division of Education, Portland State College, 1961. 72 pages.
This guide contains a chapter of 10 pages devoted specifically to the IMC.

Department of Audiovisual Instruction. *Standards for Cataloging, Coding, and Scheduling Educational Media.* Washington, D.C.: National Education Association, 1968. 56 pages.
Contains standards for cataloging educational media and coding systems for computerized cataloging and scheduling.

Educational Facilities Laboratories. *Bricks and Mortarboards.* New York: Educational Facilities Laboratories, 1963. 168 pages.
The chapter on libraries, pages 69–98, describes modern college libraries of today and plans for the future.

Educational Facilities Laboratories. *Profiles of Significant Schools: High Schools, 1962.* New York: Educational Facilities Laboratories, 1961. 88 pages.
Chapter 4 illustrates and describes modern IMCs.

Ellsworth, Ralph E., and Hobart D. Wagener. *The School Library.* New York: Educational Facilities Laboratories, 1963. 143 pages. A description of facilities for independent study in the secondary school.

Erickson, Carlton W. *Administering Instructional Media Programs.* New York: Macmillan, 1968. 660 pages.
This source book for media directors contains guidelines for developing an IMC, applications of media to instruction, and examples of current programs.

Hicks, Warren B., and Alma May Tillin. *Developing Multi-Media Libraries.* New York: R. R. Bowker, 1970. 250 pages.
How to adapt library routines and procedures to new media.

Howard, Eugene, and Roger W. Bardwell. *How to Organize a Non-Graded School.* Successful School Management/Administration Series. Englewood Cliffs, N.J.: Prentice-Hall, 1966. 64 pages.
Pages 40–46 discuss facilities for independent study.

Lineberry, William P., ed. *New Trends in the Schools.* The Reference Shelf, vol. 39, no. 2. New York: H. W. Wilson, 1967. 211 pages.
The new business-government thrust in education is discussed on pages 176–80.

Mahar, Mary H., ed. *The School Library as a Materials Center.* Proceedings of a conference sponsored by the U.S. Department of Health, Education, and Welfare in Washington, D.C., May 16–18, 1962. Washington, D.C.: U.S. Government Printing Office, 1963. 84 pages.
The educational needs of librarians and teachers in administering and using the IMC are discussed.

Michaelis, John U., Ruth H. Grossman, and Lloyd F. Scott. *New Designs for the Elementary School Curriculum.* New York: McGraw-Hill, 1967. 428 pages.
Teaching strategies and instructional media are discussed on pages 402–3 and 411–12. Suggestions for instructional media in a foreign language are given on pages 147–48.

Minor, E. O., and Harvey R. Frye. *Techniques for Producing Visual Instructional Media.* New York: McGraw-Hill, 1970. 305 pages.
Simplified mounting and preserving techniques for a variety of materials are illustrated and discussed.

National Education Association Project on Instruction. *Schools for the Sixties.* New York: McGraw-Hill, 1964. 146 pages.
At least one IMC is recommended for every school system in this report.

New Hampshire Audio-Visual Association. *Planning Audio-Visual Facilities for New School Buildings.* Concord, N.H.: New Hampshire Audio-Visual Association, 1963. 16 pages.
Pages 11–15 are devoted to the IMC. A checklist containing 26 items is included.

Peterson, Carl H. *Effective Team Teaching: The Easton Area High School Program.* Englewood Cliffs, N.J.: Prentice-Hall, 1967. 216 pages.
Practical suggestions for using multimedia are scattered throughout the book.

Prostano, Emanuel T. *School Media Programs: Case Studies in Management.* Metuchen, N.J.: Scarecrow Press, 1970. 200 pages.
Problems faced in developing and operating school media centers.

Sullivan, Peggy, ed. *Realization: The Final Report of the Knapp*

School Libraries Project. Chicago: American Library Association, 1968. 368 pages.

Reports on demonstration schools and teacher education programs.

Trump, J. Lloyd, and Dorsey Baynham. *Focus on Change: Guide to Better Schools.* Chicago: Rand McNally, 1961. 147 pages.

Dr. Trump recommends the use of a multimedia approach to independent study and suggests this be accomplished in several "learning resources centers" in each building.

Weisgerber, Robert A., ed. *Instructional Process and Media Innovation.* Chicago: Rand McNally, 1968. 569 pages.

An explanation of how media may be integrated into the instructional process.

ARTICLES

Alonso, Lou. "IMC Network Report," *Exceptional Children,* 34 (February, 1968), 461–66.

Discusses material for educators and administrators of visually handicapped children.

"A New A-V Technology for Wide-Angled Learning," *American School and University,* 39 (April, 1967), 23–27+.

Describes the blackboard-by-wire, the electrowriter, an encyclopedia on filmstrips, and a complete A-V center.

"Are Study Carrels Practical in Elementary Schools?" *School Management,* 7 (June, 1963), 55–57.

The IMCs of two elementary schools in Shaker Heights, Ohio, are described.

Beggs, David W., III. "Organization Follows Use . . . The Instructional Materials Center," *Audiovisual Instruction,* 9 (November, 1964), 602–4.

The author explains why an IMC is needed in a modern school.

Beggs, David W., III, and James Olivero. "A Place Out of Space . . . The Independent Study Carrel . . . and a Variety of Studies in Lakeview High School, Decatur, Illinois," *NASSP Bulletin,* 46 (January, 1962), 193–202.

The use and arrangement of study carrels.

Brick, E. Michael. "Learning Centers: The Key to Personalized Instruction," *Audiovisual Instruction,* 12 (October, 1967), 786–92.

Classroom and learning center functions are integrated to cope with the knowledge explosion and to provide individualized instruction. Diagrams and photographs enhance the readability.

Buehler, Ronald G. "How to Help Your Teachers Use the New Media," *The Nation's Schools,* 70 (July, 1962), 41–46.

The IMC in Grosse Pointe, Michigan.

Cardinelli, Charles F. "Effective Use of the Resources Center," *NASSP Bulletin,* 50 (September, 1966), 49–57.

Treats these aspects of the learning resources center: facilities, equipment, materials; utilization and administration; cooperative effort; and evaluation.

Carioti, Frank V. "Resource Center Uses Showcase Technics," *Nation's Schools,* 77 (March, 1966), 91–93.

The library-resource center at Chicago's South Shore High School will put its services on display through glass enclosures and functional segregation of facilities.

Costley, C. E. "Five Essentials in a Large City Program," *Audiovisual Instruction,* 5 (May, 1960), 134–35, 148.

A description of the teaching materials center in Oklahoma City. Included in the center are a curriculum library, a graphic and picture display area, a film library, a recording studio, a preview room, an equipment demonstration area, and darkroom facilities.

Dale, Edgar. "Electronic Education," *Ohio Schools,* 46 (January, 1968), 20–22+.

Discusses how and when to combine the use of electronic media with the live teacher.

Dane, Chase. "School Library as an Instructional Materials Center," *Peabody Journal of Education,* 41 (September, 1963), 81–85.

The author answers two questions: (1) What is meant by the library as a materials center? (2) Why has this change come about? He states: "Librarians are discovering that teachers and students want information, and they don't care whether this information is in a film or tape recording or a book, just so they can find it when they need it."

Darling, Richard L. "Changing Facilities for Libraries," *American School Board Journal,* 153 (December, 1966), 23–25.

How to design and equip a library to make it a comprehensive instructional media center.

Doyle, Leila. "Central Processing," *Instructor,* 75 (November, 1965), 67, 82, 84.

Central processing helps the IMC.

Doyle, Leila Ann. "Something New Has Been Added to the Library," *Childhood Education*, 43 (October, 1966), 64–68.

The library is a service center for children and teachers.

Eatough, Clair L. "What Tomorrow's Library Will Look Like," *Nation's Schools*, 77 (March, 1966), 107–9.

Tomorrow's library will be a Knowledge Resource Center with these three media: traditional, disposable, and audiovisual.

Emmerling, Frank C. "Salt for Education," *Educational Leadership*, 21 (January, 1964), 231–33.

How an IMC has improved education at the Peabody Laboratory School, The Woman's College of Georgia.

Fite, Robert E. "Is the Audiovisual Coordinator a Full-Fledged Professional Partner?" *Audiovisual Instruction*, 15 (May, 1970), 38–39.

A description of the discrepancy between the activities of the audio-visual coordinator and his performance as perceived by teachers.

Ford, Harry J. "The Instructional Resources Center," *Audiovisual Instruction*, 7 (October, 1962), 524–26.

The IMC in South Hills High School, Covina, California.

Fortado, Robert J., Edward G. Holley, and Louise Stull. "Some Materials Centers in the Midwest—A Further Look," *Journal of Teacher Education*, 14 (March, 1963), 80–86.

A survey of several midwest teacher training institutions and their nearby public schools shows that libraries contain little except printed materials.

Fulton, William R. "Developing a Self-Evaluating Instrument for Appraising Educational Media Programs," *Audiovisual Instruction*, 11 (January, 1966), 39–41.

Describes in detail an instrument for evaluating educational media programs.

Gandt, Karl O. "The Trump Plan Is Still Our Long Suit," *Nation's Schools*, 79 (April, 1967), 84.

The innovative program at Ridgewood High, Norridge, Illinois, centers on a 31,000-square-foot instructional media center.

Gehrke, Maurice N. "Starting a Graphic Service in an Instructional Materials Center," *Audiovisual Instruction*, 13 (April, 1968), 360–63.

The center's main function is to help instructors improve classroom communication through the use of new teaching devices, instructional activities and services.

Giesy, John P. "A Working Relationship," *Audiovisual Instruction,* 10 (November, 1965), 706–8.
The relationship between the central IMC and school IMCs in Flint, Michigan.

Glenn, Magdalene. "Organizing A Materials Center," *National Elementary Principal,* 40 (January, 1961), 28–30.
How the College Avenue School, Athens, Georgia, developed a materials center.

"Good Hope Counts on Variety for Multimedia Learning," *Nation's Schools,* 81 (May, 1968), 60–61.
The core of the Good Hope Intermediate School in Mechanicsburg, Pennsylvania, is an instructional media center to serve humanities, science, and cultural arts.

Guerin, David V. "Media's Influence on Design," *Audiovisual Instruction,* 10 (February, 1965), 95–97.
New media and new methods influence school design.

Hall, Sedley D. "The Instructional Materials Center," *The Elementary School Journal,* 44 (January, 1964), 210–13.
A comparison of centralized and decentralized IMCs.

Hartz, Frederic R. "Planning School Libraries for Independent Study," *Clearing House,* 40 (November, 1965), 144–48.
The author offers a four-point program for analyzing the adequacy of high school libraries to meet the needs of pupils engaged in independent study.

Helms, Annie Lou. "The Creative Elementary School Library as a Materials Center," *Wilson Library Bulletin,* 37 (October, 1962), 161–63, 184.
A description of the materials centers in the elementary schools of Bay County, Florida.

Hyer, Anna L. "Setting Quantitative Standards," *Audiovisual Instruction,* 6 (December, 1961), 506–10.
Quantitative standards for collections of instructional materials.

Jacobs, James W. "Organizing Instructional Materials Services at the System Level," *ALA Bulletin,* 62 (February, 1968), 148–52.
Suggestions for organizing instructional materials so that they relate effectively to processes of teaching and learning.

Jameson, Leonella. "Changing over to Materials Centers," *Instructor,* 74 (November, 1964), 56, 57, 71.
How the Kalamazoo, Michigan, elementary schools are gradually changing their libraries into instructional materials centers.

Knade, Oscar. "A Library is to Serve," *Elementary English,* 41 (March, 1964), 289–92.

An elementary school principal examines the services of the school library and explains the advantages of the IMC concept.

Krohn, Mildred L. "Learning and the Learning Center," *Educational Leadership,* 21 (January, 1964), 217–22.

The IMCs at Lomond and Ludlow Elementary Schools in Shaker Heights, Ohio, are described.

Lacy, Grace. "C U E—an Experiment in the Humanities," *ALA Bulletin,* 60 (October, 1966), 918–22.

The part that the newer media play in Project C U E, which stands for Cultural Understanding in Education.

Lawler, William J., and Eugene Edwards. "The Instructional Resources Center," *Audiovisual Instruction,* 7 (October, 1962), 545–50.

The IMC at Olympia High School serves Greece Central School District No. 1, Rochester, New York.

Lee, Montrose. "A New Concept in Elementary Service Library," *Audiovisual Instruction,* 10 (November, 1965), 710–11.

Children at the Williams School in Gary, Indiana, enjoy the use of many media.

Lembo, Diane. "Your Library can be the Exciting Nerve Center of your School," *Grade Teacher,* 83 (November, 1965), 92–93, 124–27.

As a natural communications hub, the school library is ideally suited to serve as a central clearing house for all teaching materials.

Matthew, Archie, and Jim Potts. "Individualize Media," *Audiovisual Instruction,* 11 (January, 1966), 42–44.

A report of the research and materials center at Lake Oswego, Oregon: how it acquaints teachers with its facilities, what it does, and how well it works.

McCarthy, James J. "IMC Network Report," *Exceptional Children,* 34 (April, 1968), 627–29.

Describes the help that teachers of children with learning disabilities can get from special education IMCs.

McGinniss, Dorothy A. "Developing Learning Resources Centers in Secondary Schools," *NASSP Bulletin,* 46 (December, 1962), 12–15.

The author thinks of the IMC in terms of four E's: Economy, Efficiency, Excellence, and Enrichment.

McGuire, Alice Brooks. "The School Librarian: A New Image," *Educational Leadership,* 21 (January, 1964), 227–30.
Why the librarian must become more flexible.

Mesedahl, Leroy K. "The IMC: Contribution to Individualized Instruction," *Audiovisual Instruction,* 10 (November, 1965), 704–5.
Two elementary schools in Duluth, Minnesota, adopt the IMC concept.

Miles, Bruce, and Virginia McJenkin. "IMC's: A Dialogue," *Audiovisual Instruction,* 10 (November, 1965), 688–91.
A librarian and an A-V specialist discuss instructional materials centers.

Miller, Albert Jay. "Education in Depth Through the Learning Center," *Pennsylvania School Journal,* 115 (April, 1967), 400–2.
The teacher and the librarian cooperatively structure a systematic plan for the use of relevant media to meet the teaching and learning needs.

Miller, Robert H. "The Media Specialists: Broward County, Florida," *Audiovisual Instruction,* 12 (February, 1967), 132–37.
A description of the organization, materials, and services of the learning resources department.

Miller, William C. "What is a Materials Center?" *Library Journal,* 85 (November 15, 1960), 17–20.
The author answers 16 frequently asked questions pertaining to the IMC.

Mitch, E. Dale. "This is Lomond School," *Instructor,* 74 (June, 1965), 47–49, 71, 72.
How independent study skills are taught and used in the intermediate grades.

Mitchell, Boyd. "Evaluative Criteria for College Instructional Materials Center," *Audiovisual Instruction,* 10 (September, 1965), 572–73.
A check list for IMCs.

Moore, Daniel." A School of Education Organizes Its Resources for Learning," *Audiovisual Instruction,* 10 (November, 1965), 700–2.
A description of the educational resources center at Western Michigan University.

Ogston, Thomas J. "Individualized Instruction: Changing the Role of the Teacher," *Audiovisual Instruction,* 13 (April, 1968), 243–48.
The most striking aspects of the Duluth Chester Park School's approach to individualized instruction are the physical layout of the building and the audiovisual equipment.

Olshin, George M. "IMC Network Report," *Exceptional Children*, 34 (October, 1967), 137–41.

Gives the locations and outlines the work of the 14 regional special education instructional materials centers funded by the U.S. Office of Education.

Olshin, George M. "Special Education Instructional Materials Center Program," *Exceptional Children*, 34 (March, 1968), 515–19.

Reviews activities and progress made to date.

Pate, Billy K. "Beginning an Instructional Materials Center," *Michigan Education Journal*, 41 (February 1, 1964), 30–31.

The IMC at Bryant Junior High School, Livonia, Michigan.

Preston, Ellinor G. "The Librarian Sees His Role in the Materials Center," *Educational Leadership*, 21 (January, 1964), 214–16, 271–72.

The challenge and the opportunity for the librarian in the instructional materials center.

Printz, Michael. "High School Library Plus," *NEA Journal*, 57 (February, 1968), 29–30.

Demonstration centers in two Topeka, Kansas, high schools are adequately staffed and provided with microfilm, recordings, films, art prints, transparencies, a stereo system, and books.

Reid, Chandos. "The Instructional Materials Center—A Service Center for Teachers," *The High School Journal*, 44 (November, 1960), 59–65.

The author points out 10 essential tasks for the efficient IMC.

Reid, William R. "IMC Network Report," *Exceptional Children*, 34 (November, 1967), 203–5.

Describes the deaf education package, film loops, picture wheels, and other materials provided in the Rocky Mountain Special Education Instructional Materials Center.

Richard, Francine. "Project Uplift," *Illinois Education*, 55 (May, 1967), 394–98.

Project Uplift is a multimedia approach to coordination, enrichment, and updating of the curriculum in the areas of language arts, reading, social studies, and science.

Richardson, Joe A., and Donald G. Carvelti. "Junior High Program Lets Slow and Fast Students Take Time for Independent Study," *Nation's Schools*, 79 (February, 1967), 74–76+.

Winnetka believes that independent study occurs when a student is in a setting where he can find and use all kinds of instructional materials.

Riley, C. William, Ella A. Schrock, and Betty Jane Lahman. "The Library and the Arts," *Theory into Practice*, 6 (February, 1967), 23–26.

An elementary school in Shaker Heights, Ohio, provides experiences in music and art by means of multimedia.

Ruark, Henry C., Jr. "It's IMC for 1963," *Educational Screen and Audiovisual Guide*, 42 (December, 1963), 674–80.

The IMC concept and the use of TV, film, and other media.

Saltzman, Stanley D. "Instructional Materials Center: The Hub of Learning," *Audiovisual Instruction*, 12 (October, 1967), 802–4.

Describes the staffing, objectives, media and materials, and leadership of the instructional media center in Farmingdale, New York. Diagrams are included.

"School Library Designed as a Materials Center," *Overview*, 1 (January, 1960), 92–93.

Pictures and description of North Central High School IMC, Washington Township, Marion County, Indiana.

Schuster, Marjorie. "City Schools and Federal Funds: Report from Cleveland," *National Elementary Principal*, 46 (January, 1967), 25–26.

Lists the programs in effect in Cleveland's new supplementary education center.

Shores, Louis. "The Medium School," *Phi Delta Kappan*, 40 (February, 1967), 285–88.

Mr. Shores foresees a "medium school" in the twenty-first century, in which the curriculum will be organized around the IMC.

Singer, Ira J. "Reducing the Research-to-Practice Gap," *Audiovisual Instruction*, 8 (November, 1963), 652–55.

Nine school districts pool their resources to support a learning resources and teacher training center in western New York.

Sleeman, Phillip J., and Robert Goff. "The Instructional Materials Center: Dialogue or Discord?" *A-V Communication Review*, 15 (Summer, 1967), 160–68.

Reviews the major functions of the IMC, pointing up hopes, promises, and controversies; and gives guidelines for future action.

Spring, Bernard P. "Plug-In Schools: Next Step in Educational Design?" *Architectural Forum*, 170 (August, 1963), 68–73.

Independent study and electronic study carrels in Michigan's Grand Valley State College.

Sylvester, Robert. "Four Steps to a Learning Center!" *Instructor*, 76 (June, 1967), 73–84.

Follows a teacher through a six-weeks summer institute, where she learned the duties of an instructional materials specialist.

Taylor, Kenneth I. "How to Plan and Equip an Instructional Materials Center," *Nation's Schools*, 67 (January, 1961), 53–60.

Mr. Taylor presents all of his material in a question-answer format. His concluding statement is "The quality of service provided to students is always a measure of successful design."

Taylor, Kenneth I. "Instructional Materials Center," *Nation's Schools*, 66 (December, 1960), 45–50.

Tha author answers a series of questions pertaining to the philosophy and organization of an IMC.

Taylor, Kenneth I. "Instructional Materials Centers and Programs," *North Central Association Quarterly*, 40 (Fall, 1965), 214–21.

Discusses these facets of the instructional media center: the concept, available standards, development and qualitative evaluation of the materials program.

Taylor, Kenneth I. "The Instructional Materials Center: A Theory Underlying Its Development," *Wisconsin Library Bulletin*, (September–October, 1967), 289–94. Reprinted in *Wilson Library Bulletin*, 43 (October, 1968), 165–68.

The premise of the theory is that the basic function of an IMC is to support schoolwide creative inquiry.

Tenhaken, Richard. "Educational Center Provides Variety," *American School Board Journal*, 154 (April, 1967), 39–41.

Explains the architectural design of the educational centers in schools in Warren County, New York.

Theodores, James L. "A New, but Much Used, Multi-Media Center, *American School and University*, 38 (April, 1966), 28–30.

One unique feature of the schools in Scarsdale, New York, is a multimedia library with 100 electronically equipped study carrels.

Toole, Martin J., and Peter Wendrychowicz. "How We Set Up Our Resource Center," *Grade Teacher*, 84 (November, 1966), 111+.

The resource center at Mahwah, New Jersey, provides materials, people, and places to implement instruction.

Tozier, Virginia. "The Child and the Library Center," *Educational Leadership*, 21 (January, 1964), 223–26, 261.

An interesting description of a dynamic IMC in the Central Park Road Elementary School, Plainview, New York.

Trenholme, A. K. "The Elementary Instructional Materials Center," *Audiovisual Instruction*, 9 (November, 1964), 620–21.

A floor plan of the Sitton Elementary School IMC in Portland, Oregon, with a short explanation of the operation.

Trump, J. Lloyd. "Independent Study Centers: Their Relation to the Central Library," *NASSP Bulletin,* 50 (January, 1966), 45–51.

Divides the learning resources center into the area for study and the area for more active work; tells how both areas are used and supervised.

Walker, Robert. "Space and Scholarship; the New Chicago Teachers College-North," *Audiovisual Instruction,* 8 (April, 1963), 202–5.

This college aims at providing space and technology to fill every instructional requirement in the preparation of modern teachers.

Ward, M. T. "Teachers Are Using MM Centers," *The Instructor,* 77 (June–July, 1968), 120.

The library-media center in an elementary school in Wichita, Kansas, is a step towards the goal of individualizing instruction.

"What Your District Can Do About School Libraries," *School Management,* 8 (April, 1964), 93–102.

How three school districts (Longmeadow, Massachusetts; Deerfield, Illinois; Melbourne, Florida) upgraded their facilities to meet the demands of the curriculum.

Wheeler, Robert C. "IMC Concept Grows Here," *Wisconsin Journal of Education,* 100 (November, 1967), 12–14.

A summary of the intended function of an instructional media center and its personnel.

Whitaker, W. F. "Corridors Circle Junior High Instructional Materials Center," *Nation's Schools,* 80 (July, 1967), 32.

All students in an Athens, Tennessee, junior high are scheduled into the instructional media center.

White, Frederick A. "An Audiovisual Demonstration Project," *Wisconsin Journal of Education,* 99 (January, 1967), 24–25.

Describes a demonstration unit which gives teachers an in-depth experience in utilizing the full staff of an ideal audiovisual center.

Williams, Philip. "A Materials Centre for Special Education," *Educational Research,* 9 (November, 1966), 53–55.

Diagrams a program for material evaluation and explains the services provided by the materials center for special education at the University of Wisconsin.

Williamson, Walter W. "Developing an Instructional Materials Center in the Mount Royal School," *Educational Leadership,* 25 (November, 1967), 167 +.

The author gives a detailed account of how a multimedia instructional center was established in an inner city school in Baltimore.

Wyman, Raymond. "The Instructional Materials Center: Whose Empire?" *Audiovisual Instruction*, 12 (February, 1967), 114–16.
Describes the material and human resources needed to establish an instructional media center. Includes diagrams.

Zazzaro, Joanne. "They've Almost Invented Instant Learning," *American School Board Journal*, 156 (September, 1968), 10–14.
The Oak Park, Illinois, High School IMC includes a computer retrieval system.

Notes

CHAPTER 2

1. Ministry of Education, *The School Library* (London, England: Ministry of Education, 1952), p. 12.
2. American Association of School Librarians, *Standards for School Library Programs* (Chicago: American Library Association, 1960), p. 11.
3. NEA Project on Instruction, *Schools for the Sixties* (New York: McGraw-Hill, 1963), p. 98.
4. Louis Shores, "Enter the Materials Center," *ALA Bulletin*, XLIX (June, 1955), 285.
5. *Ibid.*, p. 288.
6. National Study of Secondary School Evaluation, *Evaluative Criteria* (Washington, D.C.: The Association, 1960), p. 257.
7. *Standards for School Library Programs*, p. 12.
8. "The Instructional Materials Center," *Overview*, III (July, 1962), 28.
9. Margaret Nicholsen, "IMC," *School Libraries*, XIII (March, 1964), 39–43.
10. Frances Henne, "School Libraries as Centers for Learning Experiences," *NEA Journal*, LI (March, 1962), 98.
11. NEA Project on Instruction, *Schools for the Sixties*, p. 99.
12. John Goodlad, *Planning and Organizing for Teaching* (Washington, D.C.: NEA, 1963), p. 125.

CHAPTER 3

1. John W. Gardner, *Excellence: Can We Be Equal and Excellent Too?* (New York: Harper & Row, 1961).
2. Ellwood F. Cubberley, *The History of Education* (Boston: Houghton-Mifflin, 1948).
3. R. Freeman Butts, *A Cultural History of Western Education* (2nd ed.; New York: McGraw-Hill, 1955).
4. Monica Kiefer, *American Children through Their Books, 1700–1835* (Philadelphia: University of Pennsylvania Press, 1948).
5. Ralph S. Tyler, *Basic Principles of Curriculum and Instruction* (Chicago: University of Chicago Press, 1950).
6. Ralph E. Ellsworth and Hobart D. Wagener, *The School Library:*

Facilities for Independent Study in the Secondary School (New York: Educational Facilities Laboratories, 1963).

7. Allen H. Barton and David E. Wilder, "Research and Practice in the Teaching of Reading: A Progress Report," *Innovation in Education,* ed. Matthew B. Miles (New York: Teachers College, Columbia University, 1964).

8. Benjamin S. Bloom, ed., *Taxonomy of Educational Objectives, Handbook 1: Cognitive Domain* (New York: Longmans, Green, 1956).

9. David R. Krathwohl, et al., *Taxonomy of Educational Objectives, Handbook 2: Affective Domain* (New York: David McKay, 1964).

10. Nelson B. Henry, ed., *The Measurement of Understanding,* Forty-fifth Yearbook of the National Society for the Study of Education, Part 1 (Chicago: University of Chicago Press, 1946).

11. Helen M. Carpenter, ed., *Skill Development in Social Studies,* Thirty-third Yearbook (Washington, D.C.: National Council for the Social Studies, 1963).

12. John Dewey, *Experience and Education* (New York: Macmillan, 1938).

CHAPTER 4

1. American Library Association and American Association of School Librarians, *School Libraries for Today and Tomorrow: Functions and Standards* (Chicago: American Library Association, 1945).

2. American Association of School Librarians, *Standards for School Library Programs* (Chicago: American Library Association, 1960).

3. American Association of School Librarians, *Standards for School Media Programs* (Chicago: American Library Association, 1969).

CHAPTER 5

1. NEA Project on Instruction, *Schools for the Sixties* (New York: McGraw-Hill, 1963).

CHAPTER 6

1. Ed Minor and Harvey R. Frye, *Techniques for Producing Visual Instructional Media* (New York: McGraw-Hill, 1970).

CHAPTER 7

1. Council on Library Resources, *Third Annual Report* (Washington, D.C.: 1959), p. 13.

2. "Electronics," *Standard & Poor's Industry Survey,* September 24, 1964, Table 19, p. E24.

3. "Knowledge Explosion," *New York Times,* May 26, 1963.

4. "Knowledge, the Biggest Growth Industry of Them All, *Fortune,* November, 1964.

5. LeRoy R. Lindeman, "A Proposed Audio-Visual Program for the State of Utah" (Doctoral Dissertation, Brigham Young University, 1965).

6. *Ibid.*

CHAPTER 8

1. American Association of School Librarians, *Standards for School Library Programs* (Chicago: American Library Association, 1960), pp. 25, 53–55.

2. American Association of School Librarians, *Standards for School Media Programs* (Chicago: American Library Association, 1969), p. 12.

3. *Ibid.*, p. 16.

4. *Standards for School Library Programs*, pp. 96–99.

5. *Ibid.*, p. 102.

6. "A statement prepared by the Joint AASL-ACRL-DAVI Committee" (1958), reprinted in *Standards for School Library Programs*, pp. 59–62.

CHAPTER 10

1. Nancy Larrick, "Textbooks and Teaching Aids," *PTA Magazine*, LVII (December, 1963), 4–6.

CHAPTER 12

NOTE: The photographs in this chapter are by Michael Mittison, and the graphic art by Joyce Peckham.

1. See Chapter 3 of this volume. See also "The Instructional Materials Center: A Theory Underlying Its Development," *Wisconsin Library Bulletin* (September–October, 1967), 289–94. Reprinted in *Wilson Library Bulletin*, 43 (October, 1968), pp. 165–68.

2. Jessica Holmes and Boyd Geer, *Instructional Materials Centers and A-V Library Responsibilities* (Madison Public Schools, 1968). 57fr filmstrip, 12 min tape, 16 p manual.

CHAPTER 13

1. John Kenneth Galbraith, *The Liberal Hour* (Boston: Houghton-Mifflin, 1960).

Index